To my family, especially my mother and father,
Dorothea and Alphonse, whose quiet life and
fierce devotion made all the difference

Contents

How to Unscramble Your Nest Egg

A Fresh Approach to Personal Abundance and Building Real Home Ownership

JOHN J. CUNNINGHAM

CONTEMPORARY BOOKS

CHICAGO

Library of Congress Cataloging-in-Publication Data

Cunningham, John J.
    How to unscramble your nest egg : a fresh approach to
personal abundance and building real home ownership /
John J. Cunningham.
        p.   cm.
    ISBN 0-8092-3643-5 (paper)
    1. Mortgage loans—United States.   2. Prepayment of
debts—United States.   3. Saving and investment—United
States.   4. Retirement
income—United States.   I. Title.
HG2040.5.U5C86   1994
332.7'22—dc20   94-12158
                                                                  CIP

Material in Chapter 4 from *The Richest Man in Babylon* by
George S. Clason. Copyright © 1955 by George S. Clason,
renewed © 1983 by Clyde Clason. Used by permission of
Dutton Signet, a division of Penguin Books USA Inc.

Published by Contemporary Books, Inc.
Two Prudential Plaza, Chicago, Illinois 60601-6790
Manufactured in the United States of America
International Standard Book Number: 0-8092-3643-5
10   9   8   7   6   5   4   3   2   1

Preface

The long journey to this book actually started in 1982 when I was visiting my family in Philadelphia. It was one of those gray and overcast winter days, and we were sitting around the breakfast table watching my father perform his winter ritual. Every morning, my father would don my old football jacket, pull a navy cap over his ears, and break up the ice in the birdbath. After he put in fresh water and went inside, the sparrows could hardly wait to swoop down and begin their fun. As we were enjoying their exuberance that winter morning, my younger sister turned and asked my advice on refinancing her mortgage.

Eileen and her husband, Joe, had a $28,000 mortgage with an exorbitant interest rate of nearly 15 percent (remember those days?). She wanted to know whether it was a good idea to spend $3,000 in points and fees to refinance their mortgage to 11.5 percent. Naturally, I first thought in terms of how long it would take to recover the fees in lower monthly payments and all the other typical considerations. Then I had the idea that perhaps we should also evaluate the effect of applying this same $3,000 directly against the principal loan balance.

The results were astounding. This option immediately

eliminated 15 years of mortgage payments, which saved an awesome $59,000 in scheduled interest expense. That's not all. Once their mortgage was paid off 15 years early, Eileen and Joe would have the opportunity to put the ex-mortgage payments into a savings account earning (at that time) an average of 8 percent per annum. By the end of the 15 years, their investment would build to a nest egg of approximately $124,000! Needless to say, we were astounded.

Now aware of this opportunity, Eileen and Joe had a fresh choice. They could choose to refinance for a lower monthly payment, or by virtue of paying the $3,000 against principal they could keep the same monthly payment and create a future nest egg with an economic value of $124,000. Even if the money never actually makes it into the savings account but is spent on tuition, elderly parents, and vacations instead, these 15 years retain the same economic value because it's their own money, not borrowed funds, that's being spent. As it happened, and partially because they could afford the current monthly payment, Joe and Eileen chose to accelerate the $3,000 of principal and eliminate the 15 years of mortgage payments. Furthermore, as it later happened, when interest rates fell to 10 percent they refinanced to a 10-year mortgage and also lowered their monthly payment. Moreover, Eileen and Joe slashed away another 5 years of mortgage payments and increased their potential nest egg to an economic value of more than $200,000.

As delighted as I was for Eileen and Joe, I was also mystified. How could they eliminate $59,000 of interest expense, even with an interest rate of 15 percent, with $3,000? After all, 15 percent of $3,000 is only $450.

When I finally discovered the answer, I was amazed at its simplicity. And no, the answer isn't that the lender stacked all the interest in the front as many people believe. The real answer is that there are two sides to the mortgage coin. One side reflects the annual cost of managing *debt*. The other side reflects the cost of buying *equity* ownership.

If your intent is to simply manage debt by striving for the lowest monthly payment, the annual interest *rate* is indeed considered the true cost of a mortgage. This may be called the debt perspective. However, if your objective is to build real equity ownership, the other way to measure your mortgage is on the basis of interest *expense*. In other words, you need to think in terms of *cash*, not percentages. Viewing a mortgage in terms of cash and interest expense can be called the equity perspective.

Not understanding the difference between these two sides of the coin is the reason I didn't understand how Eileen and Joe could eliminate $59,000 of interest expense. I was comparing a debt orange to an equity apple. I was trying to apply a 15 percent debt rate against what was essentially an equity consideration. Instead of using a percentage, I should have been thinking in terms of cash. When I examined the actual repayment schedule from this perspective I could see that it called for an average of *$55 in interest expense for every $1 of principal* during the first 5 years of their mortgage. This means that Eileen and Joe's true cost of buying ownership during this period was 5,500 percent! The good news was that it also meant that every $1 of principal acceleration eliminated as much as $55 of scheduled interest expense, which was a 5,500 percent return on investment. Eureka! The mystery was solved.

But that's not the end of the story. Other things were happening. The equity perspective seemed so *right . . .* right now. So did the idea of creating new choices and reconsidering the trade-offs between a lower monthly payment and a potential nest egg. Why?

When I stepped back and looked at the larger picture—changes in the economy, our lifestyle, strains on the government, home appreciation, the retirement system, and other trends—I realized that building equity, preserving cash, and recapturing the treasure buried in our mortgage is more than smart. In these uncertain times, it's absolutely necessary.

Thus, in this book I want to share more than the "how to" of principal acceleration. I want to share the "why." I'd like to retrace my steps and include you in the journey. Like a pleasant afternoon of enjoying the scenery from a rowboat, witnessing changes in the economic landscape of this country will help you understand the purpose of building equity and the role of principal acceleration in our changing world.

As fascinating as was my journey, I've never lost sight of the fact that this book isn't just a "how-to" manual on mortgages. Its *real* purpose is to help you create the financial security, personal freedom, and peace of mind that you deserve. Nothing else could be more important.

Introduction

We can no longer borrow ourselves rich. Financial security now belongs to those who build real equity ownership and a nest egg of their own. For most people there is no bigger opportunity to do this than through their home investment.

The shift from a debt management clime to an equity-building clime will be long-lived. It's part of a long-term trend that includes the transition to an economy based on information and technology, the demise of lifelong careers and secure pensions, soft appreciation, and the passage of the baby boom generation. There is no stopping these changes, and there is no value in trying to swim against the tide. Rather, we must use an equity-wise strategy to move in harmony with these changes, reduce our vulnerability, and garner strength as we await the eventual prosperity of the new economy.

Building equity and preserving cash does not, however, mean banning debt altogether. That would be impractical as well as impossible. It does mean shifting from *lazy* debt to *hardworking* debt. Lazy debt is loaded with interest expense. Monthly payments do little more than support a large loan balance, lose time, and hope for appreciation. In contrast, hardworking debt is packed with principal. Its monthly payments build equity ownership, repay the loan in the shortest possible time, and liberate money for use as a nest egg. This is good, smart debt. Shifting to a strategy marked by smart, hardworking debt is the way to financial success in the 1990s.

How to Unscramble Your Nest Egg applies this equity-wise strategy in two practical ways. First, it enables you to make an informed decision in selecting a home mortgage. It provides rare insights into the equity aspects of a mortgage. Everyone understands mortgages from a debt perspective—interest rate, monthly payments, repayment term, and so forth—but few people know anything about the purchasing power of their monthly payment, the vast difference between an interest *rate* and interest *expense*, and the trade-off between their initial gain in borrowing power and the total opportunity loss for that gain. Evaluating a prospective mortgage from both the debt and equity perspectives gives you the confidence that you're making the best decision possible.

The second way this book applies the equity-wise strategy is by explaining how to transform an existing lazy mortgage into a smart, hardworking one. The name of this strategy is *principal acceleration*. Although descended from an older method known as *mortgage prepayment*, principal acceleration is unique in tailoring its strategy to each homeowner's individual mortgage. In particular its strategy is customized according to the purchasing power, true cost, and initial gain/opportunity loss criteria of the equity perspective. This is the reason a strategic principal acceleration plan is three times more effective than conventional prepayment.

In addition to eliminating lazy debt and enabling the monthly payment to build equity ownership, principal acceleration offers an equally important benefit—it's the source of your nest egg for the future. Once money that was previously earmarked for payments on lazy-debt mortgage loans has been liberated, it can be redirected into your nest egg. You may be surprised and delighted to realize that, by performing this simple act, you *already* earn enough income to enjoy the financial security and peace of mind you deserve. Investing it in equity rather than debt is the key.

This book is divided into three parts. Part I discusses the emotional, economic, and financial reasons for building real home ownership and preserving cash. For instance, the first chapter, "Sanctuary," reminds you how equity ownership protects the peace, sanctity, and security of your home. Chapter 3, "Home Economics," guides you in selecting a mortgage from an equity-wise perspective. Part II is concerned with the how-to aspects of principal acceleration. Anyone capable enough to endure the qualification process for acquiring a new mortgage will find principal acceleration a snap. Part III is devoted to related equity and principal acceleration topics, such as the mythical benefits of debt. Another chapter in this section guides you through all the housekeeping chores with your lender.

Taken altogether, *How to Unscramble Your Nest Egg* is more than a book about mortgages or arithmetic techniques. It's an overall philosophy—the Zen of home ownership. Throughout this book you'll encounter fairy tales, fables, poems, Buddhist riddles, natural history, famous quotes, and many other storytelling vehicles that reveal the timeless truths and human face of personal economics. Moreover, I know that people are less motivated by money and being smart than by reasons of the heart. Hence, it's only fitting that I start this book with a topic the heart has never forgotten, namely that home is more than a house, a possession, a financial investment—the home is a sanctuary.

PART I
EQUITY
OWNERSHIP

1
Sanctuary

The image and idea of "coming home" holds a special meaning for most of us. It resonates in our hearts and minds. It engenders a warm and safe feeling. Home is, after all, more than a house, a possession, a financial investment—home is sanctuary. No other place is so satisfying. Sanctuary offers quietude, true relaxation, and constancy. It provides a space to express our beliefs and ideals, enjoy the sweetness of life, raise a family, and experience our truest selves. It sanctifies our everyday activities and contributes to our peace of mind. Failing to find this love, peace, and joy in the outside world, people are coming home to their sanctuary.

Home is actually worth so much to our sense of well-being and happiness that the first duty of every homeowner is to safeguard the sanctuary against all threats, including economic ones. Even though it may be our biggest investment and the object of our largest hope for financial profit, we must resist the temptation to put our home at risk. Instead, we should build a solid foundation of real equity ownership to reduce its vulnerability to the uncertainties of an economic world.

Although this is now an economic world, nothing has

3

really changed since the time the Romans and Greeks honored the value of a home sanctuary. Indeed, life remains exactly the same.

Ancient Passages

Where there is love, *there* is home. Home is sanctuary. Sanctuary is where our spirits are nourished and refreshed. Joseph Campbell, author of *The Power of Myth* and the landmark *Hero with a Thousand Faces*, had sanctuary in mind when he said that everyone needs a space where he can forget what he owes and what anyone owes him, the chores yet to be accomplished, the obligations yet to be fulfilled, the challenges at work, the mistakes he regrets, the past and future, and everything else but his connection to that other self—that other quality of being that every person usually glimpses only in times of deep love or great sorrow. At these times our outer public self disappears and we have a direct encounter with our inner private self. This is our truest self, the self that knows the real meaning of "coming home."

Sanctuary also awakens a love and appreciation for ourselves. Like swans, afloat and asleep outside the temple gate, sanctuary is the tolling bell that awakens us to the beauty within. Awakening to this joy and beauty is not an egotistical pursuit; it's an appreciation for the higher and more noble aspects of being human. No matter our station in life—whether we are single or married, rich or poor, renter or owner, young or old—our lives have purpose and dignity. Remembering this is a choice, though. Life is difficult. Choosing the joy in life over its pains and travails is essential to experiencing our true selves. A home sanctuary is host to customs, practices, traditions, and other remembrances that sanctify our everyday activities and help us make that choice. These customs and rituals add a sweetness to life.

Relaxation is yet another benefit. Chogyam Trungpa,

Tibetan teacher and author of *Sambhala, Sacred Path of the Warrior*, noted that true relaxation is not flopping in front of a TV, drinking a cocktail, taking a vacation, or pursuing other diversions. It is relaxing the mind, letting go of the anxiety, frustration, worry, concepts, and games that dominate our outer public lives. Only in our inner private lives can we truly relax. Where else but in our sanctuary can we experience this part of life?

Home is the birthplace of values that hold the fabric of society together: self-discipline, perseverance in the face of adversity, courage to challenge our doubts, faith in a positive outcome, trust in our community and neighbors, fair play with an opponent, honesty in all our dealings, scruples in not taking advantage of others, patience, generosity in sharing good fortune and abundance, loyalty, sacrificing today for a better tomorrow, hard work. The author and teacher, M. Scott Peck calls them *civilities*. They are the stuff of which heroes are made. Indeed, *how* the game is played makes all the difference in the outcome. When Michael Jordan, Joe Montana, Wayne Gretzky, and Carlton Fisk are inducted into their respective Halls of Fame, what everyone will remember is not the score of any game, but *how* they played the game. These civilities are not made on the playing field; they're born at home. You and I may never be inducted into a Hall of Fame, yet we're heroes every time we plant a garden, coach Little League, attend a civic meeting, paint a living room wall, hang a piece of art, walk the dog, host a dinner party, help the children with homework, donate to charity, celebrate the holidays, and participate in the many other daily activities of our community.

Quietude and constancy are yet additional benefits. A home sanctuary can offset the dizzying effect of change in our everyday lives. The 800th lifetime, which Alvin Toffler described in his visionary book *Future Shock*, is an excellent analogy to illustrate the pace of such change. It goes like this: if the last 50,000 years of human existence were divided into lifetimes of 62 years each, there would be approximately 800 such lifetimes. Of these, 650 were spent in caves. Only during the last 6 lifetimes did masses of people see the printed word. Only in the last 2 lifetimes has anyone, anywhere, used an electric motor. Finally, the overwhelming majority of goods we use in daily life have been developed in this last lifetime, the 800th. The hectic pace created by this swirl of change cries out for a space where we can refresh and remember our true selves.

All of these benefits, and others not mentioned, are the benefits of a sanctuary. Only at home can these enjoyments be found. Reconnecting with ourselves in a home sanctuary is not the same as being removed from the world, though. To be completely removed from information and knowledge of the outside world isn't possible or completely desirable. It's a question of balance. Within your home there is both a place for the world and a space for sanctuary.

Sanctuary, after all, is a space, not necessarily a place. A place is a physical location or piece of architecture. Any place, whether owned or rented, can be made into sanctuary space. It can be a house, multifamily dwelling, trailer, tent, cabin, or other edifice. Or it can be just a *part* of a structure; any space can be designated as sanctuary. A sanctuary can be a bathtub, a hot tub, a corner in a room, an entire room, or every room in the house but the one in which the television, radio, telephone, and fax machine are located. I have a special table on which I keep a lighted candle and a fresh flower as reminders of my sanctuary space. Mountain cabins or other remote retreats that have no telecommunication devices, and perhaps no electricity or water, often serve as sanctuary space. Joseph Campbell spent a year in one such cabin in Woodstock, New York. When he asked the farmer-landlord why electricity but not running water was installed, the farmer replied, "I don't like the kind of people it attracts."

Whatever place you designate as sanctuary space, it's vital to set aside time and space to reconnect with your true self. Sadly, however, enjoying sanctuary time and space isn't encouraged in contemporary life. Quite the opposite. We're encouraged to be more effective as economic units, not as human beings. Accordingly, creating sanctuary, and the time and space to enjoy it, requires extra effort. This challenge is not entirely new. Even if the issues were different, people throughout all history have faced the same challenge. Traditions that have developed in Western culture as a result of these efforts can serve as a model to us in the twentieth century. Many of these traditions, customs, and rituals stretch back through the Renaissance to the classical period of Greece and Rome.

Virtually all of these traditions position the woman as the keeper of the sanctuary. These traditions were not intended to limit a woman to household chores, as some would prefer, but were actually intended to give her dominion over the peace and sanctity of the home sanctuary. Hers were sacred duties, not menial tasks. Although a woman's keeper role began as part of a traditional marriage role, it now applies to all forms of living arrangements, whether those involved are married, single, divorced, widowed, or in partnership. Furthermore, the role of keeper is no longer the exclusive domain of women. In contemporary society traditional roles have since merged into a partnership where both men and women share the responsibility and help each other in safeguarding all aspects of the home sanctuary. This is especially true as it pertains to the earning and use of money to protect the space against the encroachments of the outside world.

Even though these traditions and roles have since changed, there is a great deal to be learned by tracing the origins, cultural mythology, and traditions that ordained the woman as the keeper of the sanctuary. For this purpose, the traditions of the wedding ceremony are illustrative. It's full of symbols that consecrated the woman as queen of the home. Her dominion was further established by the traditional housewarming ceremony, where the new hearth was lit by a flame from her mother's own hearth, and thus the torch was passed from generation to generation.

Wedding and Housewarming Ceremonies

In Western culture a wedding ceremony was symbolically a royal coronation when a woman was turned into a queen. She was ritually bathed and anointed with oil and perfume, and traditionally her hair was cut. She was dressed in royal-like garments, bejeweled, veiled, and crowned. She received a nuptial blessing reserved exclusively for her. Thus coronated, the queen was consecrated in her role as keeper of the sanctuary and protector of its love.

Traditionally a feast was held at the bride's father's house, after which she was escorted to her new home by a procession that included musicians, children carrying flowers, ladies-in-waiting, the priest, celebrants, the groom, and the bride's mother as torchbearer. Upon arrival a housewarming ceremony, considered as important as the wedding itself, was held to consecrate the couple's new home. This tradition extends back to the time of the ancient Greeks and Romans. The bride was first carried over the threshold so nothing of the outside world would contaminate the home. Then the newlyweds positioned themselves in front of the hearth for another exchange of vows and the housewarming ceremony.

Imagine that it's now 375 B.C., and you're attending a wedding that has just taken place in the Great Temple in Athens. The bride's name is Olympias, and the groom's is Agis. Olympias has the blond hair and blue eyes of her mother's ancestors in Macedonia. Her mother's name is Helen. Agis, whose strong profile would turn craggy in later life, has the black hair and eyes of his Greek parents. Calchas, the priest, whose white-gold beard is as dense as a sheep's coat, was also the celebrated soothsayer at the siege of Troy.

The wedding procession has reached the new home,

and Agis has just carried Olympias over the threshold. Now comes the time to exchange vows concerning the care and safekeeping of their new home: "Olympias," begins Calchas, "as queen of this home, it is your sacred duty to maintain the hearth fire as symbol of the love that binds all of us together. Do you vow to keep the hearth fire burning and never let it go out?"

"Yes, I do," replies Olympias.

"Do you promise to preserve this home as sanctuary for this love?"

"I do."

"Do you promise to maintain peace in the sanctuary and keep the fears of the world from invading it?" continues Calchas.

Again, Olympias says, "I do."

"Finally, do you promise to maintain the sanctity of the home by remembering that it is love being nourished, not just the body?"

"I do," says Olympias with a smile.

Calchas then turns to Agis and says "Agis, do you vow to protect the home sanctuary against all harm, whether man, beast, or nature, and no matter the consequences to you?"

"I do," replies Agis.

"Do you promise to secure it from the intrigues of worldly ambitions?" asks Calchas.

"I do"

"Finally, do you promise not to let the attraction of personal gain lead to gambles that put the home at risk?"

It is with firm resolve that Agis makes this final vow. "I do," he says.

"With these vows complete, I now call forth Helen, mother of the bride and queen, that she and Olympias may join hands on the torch and together light the hearth and consecrate this home sanctuary."

With a tear on the cheek of Helen and a smile brightening the face of Olympias, the flame from mother's hearth is passed to daughter's hearth, and a new sanctuary is welcomed into the community. Calchas's last official words are, "Let the music begin."

Passing the torch from generation to generation and lighting the hearth fire symbolized the transformation of a mere house into a home sanctuary. The spirit of love had come to abide in that home.

The hearth was sacred ritual fire, not a cooking fire. The phrase *mistress of hearth and home* doesn't mean chief cook; it means keeper of the sacred flame. Flame has been used to symbolize the spirit of life throughout history. Important shrines often immortalize the person they honor with an eternal flame, such as the grave of John F. Kennedy. The Olympic torch symbolizes the brotherhood of mankind. Common phrases such as *Keep the home fires burning, He's still carrying a torch for her, Home is where the heart is, Hearth and home,* and numerous other expressions recall the spirit and meaning of the hearth flame. The Latin *hearth* means "to focus." *Hearth* and *heart* share the same Latin root. The hearth fire was intended to focus attention on the love of the family.

After the hearth had been lit, the bride and groom were enthroned, where they ate from a special dish and exchanged morsels of food. Their last public ritual before retiring from the celebration was cutting the cake for the rest of the celebrants.

Keepers and Guardians

Since those ancient times, everything has changed, but nothing is different: love is home, and home is sanctuary. Responsibility for the home sanctuary is a sacred duty that has traditionally been given into the keeping of the woman or queen of the family. She is the *keeper* of the sanctuary. Being the keeper isn't a work assignment, however. It's a confirmation of her dominion over the peace and sanctity of the space. It also establishes her authority over the customs, rituals, and ceremonies that commemorate the love and spirit of the family and that signify the family's membership in the larger community.

Unfortunately, the execution of this power has never been without opposition. There are powerful forces that wish to diminish the keeper's role because it represents a power that is opposite to their own. In brief, they believe that authority, prestige, and wealth should go toward those who have the power to destroy life, not to those who create and protect life. The power to create life versus the power to destroy life is one of the quintessential struggles in all of recorded history, regardless of culture, race, religion, or era. One side believes in the spirit of life; the other side believes in the body of life. It is the heart versus the intellect. It is love versus fear. It is life versus death. It is the chalice versus the blade.

Historically, men have been associated with the blade and women with the chalice. Even so, this is not a gender issue. There have been a good number of women rulers, for instance, who have believed in the power of the sword as much as men believe in it. Witness Cleopatra; Queen Isabella of Spain; Mary, Queen of Scots; and Catherine the Great of Russia. Indeed, it's not so much a gender issue as it is an issue of conflicting beliefs. Those who honor the blade over the chalice will always challenge the keeper's role and attempt to diminish her sacred duties and responsibilities. Fear not, however. The keeper of the sanctuary is safe. It may be inevitable that the body will die, but the death of the spirit is impossible.

In ancient Greece, the keeper's heroine was the Greek goddess Hestia. (Greek gods and goddesses were considered in the same way that Christians now look to patron saints for guidance.) Hestia was the goddess of hearth and temple/home, as well as the wise woman who could be trusted for advice. Her symbol was a round hearth fire.

Hermes was the Greek god and hero for the man or king of the home. Hermes was the guide, companion, and protector of travelers, businessmen, and others engaged in commerce, exchange, secrecy, cleverness, and other activities of worldly material life. Hermes's symbol was stone pillars placed by the threshold of the home. Pillars like these can be found on the front of many important buildings today. The king's role is to secure the home against hostile outside forces, as well as to prohibit worldly ambitions from threatening the sanctuary. He is the *guardian* of the sanctuary.

Second only to raising children, safeguarding the sanctuary was and still is the primary duty of keepers and guardians. The term *safeguard* means more than protecting against immediate dangers; it implies watching over and taking precautionary measures to prevent future threats. In one-adult households, the responsibilities of both keeper and guardian fall on one person. Although the keeper may still hold the deciding vote in matters concerning the inner realm of the sanctuary, and the guardian may still hold sway over the exterior and physical structure, their traditional roles have gradually merged, and both partners are now responsible for safeguarding the sanctuary. The merging of these two roles is especially valuable in our modern world because there's an additional danger—economics.

Economics has replaced nature as the primary source of abundance in contemporary life. This is particularly true in America, where corporate capitalism is the ruling force. On the whole this has been a boon to the average American—we live better lives today than Alexander the Great or even Frederick the Great imagined possible. No longer are we dependent on nature and limited natural resources as our sole source of abundance. But an economic world also has inherent dangers. A couple of times every century the economy goes through a major transition and produces a wave of change that catches the unwary by surprise and wipes them out before they've had a chance to recover. People sometimes lose their home sanctuary because they're not prepared for such economic transitions.

Such a loss can be devastating. People must take extra precautions and initiate economic safeguards that protect the peace, sanctity, and security of the home sanctuary against this threat. This is not a new situation. Economic safeguards were probably just as important to Olympias, almost 2,400 years ago, as they are for us today.

Ancient coins, which had divine images on one side and an image of the ruler on the other, indicate that Olympias would have used money to address economic concerns, as well as concerns of the hearth. For example, she would have used money to reduce encumbrances against the home and thus provide her family with the economic peace and peace of mind that they deserved. She would have used money for activities that helped sanctify the space, not in a religious way, but in a way that recalled love and the spirit of life. Furthermore, Olympias would have removed her home from the quest for financial gain and other worldly ambitions. Her home would not have been used for possible profit, but for certain security.

So it should be with us. Money that's used to reduce encumbrances against the home, gain a regular and increasing amount of equity, and follow a strategy designed to build real home ownership, thus protecting the peace, sanctity, and security of the home sanctuary, is money well spent.

Peace

The hearth's traditional location was the threshold of a home, often in the foyer, because its symbolic function was to keep the fears of the world from entering the home and polluting the love and peace of the sanctuary. Peace is more than the absence of war, it's the complete absence of enemies or even the perception of genuine opposition. Peace is essential to a sanctuary. Without it, there is no home, just an abode for our physical bodies.

The same is true of the profanities of the world. *Profanities* is the ancient name for the events, situations, and people that instilled fear. These profanities were considered a curse on humanity. The ancient concept of the profane included anything that defiled the holy or sacred aspects of life, especially acts of hatred and physical harm. They specifically included all violence, war, murder, rape, incest, torture, slavery, plunder, crime, suicide, betrayal, and similar acts. Even their discussion or symbols, such as weapons, were banned from the home because they instilled fear indirectly. This tradition is still observed in much of the Western world. The Victorians went so far as to relegate certain topics—money, financial threats and material possessions, politics, sickness and disease, religion, race, crime and punishment, social position, and similar aspects of public life—to a special room so they wouldn't contaminate the sanctuary and the family's peace of mind; absolutely never were they to be discussed while breaking bread.

We too should be concerned about our peace of mind, and in fact the modern world demands that we take extra precautions to preserve it. The technologies that pervade modern life make this exceedingly difficult. In fact, electronics accelerate the perception of danger in the world. Fear increases correspondingly. On the hour and half hour the news invades our space and tells us of every travesty occurring in the entire world: war, famine and starvation, racial strife, religious hatred, murder, automobile accidents, personal tragedies, and all the rest. The news never stops. As soon as one situation loses its novelty, the media move on to the next newsworthy event, situation, or personality. It's easy to forget that the news is not the entire truth. Nor is it knowledge; it's not even information. It's just a fragment of a story. The author and diplomat George Kennan noted: "Fleeting, disjointed, visual glimpses of reality, flickering on and off the screen, here today and gone to-

morrow, are not the 'information' on which sound judgments can be formed." What the news does show is only a
tiny .001 percent of noteworthy incidents, which improp-
erly shape our perception of life as a dangerous experience.
It appears the entire world is divided and separated into
warring camps, and to avoid becoming victims we must
constantly be on the defensive. That's not living; that's just
surviving.

In addition to the unrelenting bombardment by the
news, our peace of mind is further threatened by telecommunications, which can invade our space at will. We're
encouraged to have a telephone in every conceivable location so our privacy can be violated at another's whim.
(Ironically, telecommunication devices are permitted to
invade our space electronically, whereas invading someone's space in person is against the law.) This electronic
power is so taken for granted that many callers get upset if
someone refuses to take their telephone call, even though
they would never walk into an office or a home without an
appointment and expect to be seen. The fact that others can
invade our privacy at their whim means they have the
ability to destroy our peace at their will.

Forfeiting the peace of our sanctuary for the sake of
"being informed" or "saving time," which are the supposed
rewards of news and telecommunications, is a mean trade-
off. As implied before, the objective isn't to be removed
from considerations of the world, but to establish a balance
between the demands of our outer public life and the truth
of our inner private lives.

Actually, the idea that every person is entitled to peace
is codified into law and extends far back into Western
history. In old England the sanctity of the king and queen's
palace extended to the dwelling place of their liege. Their
liege's home was likewise considered a palace, not a castle
per se, with the same rights and privileges. This right to
peace still exists today. It includes more than laws against
disturbing the peace (quiet). In Scotland, for instance, pun-

ishment for a crime committed in the home is more severe
than for the same crime committed outside. Similarly, in
America, the authorities must obtain a warrant signed by a
magistrate before they can invade and disturb the peace of
a household. The Declaration of Independence, the U.S.
Constitution, and the Bill of Rights express this concept as
an inalienable right. The lesson of history is that without
peace there can be no sanctuary.

To be sure, the fears of the world cannot be allowed to
invade the home and destroy the peace of the sanctuary.
Such fears also include economic fear. We're subject to
economic fear, for example, whenever our homes are
vulnerable to unpredictable swings in the economy and
housing market. Fortunately, this fear can be eliminated by
using our money wisely to reduce the liabilities and encumbrances against the home. Then, not only will we enjoy the
peace of the sanctuary, we'll also enjoy economic peace of
mind.

Sanctity

Customs, rituals, and celebrations help us remember the joy
and sweetness of life. They help sanctify everyday experiences as well as significant events. They help us remember
that a home is intended to nourish the soul, not just comfort the body. As Kahlil Gibran noted in *The Prophet*, in
"On Houses," "The house is your larger body. . . . Have you
peace? . . . Have you remembrances? . . . Have you beauty?
. . . Or, have you only comfort, that stealthy thing that enters
the house a guest, and then becomes a host, and then becomes a master? . . . Lust for comfort murders the passion
of the soul."

Customs

Customs, which are established gestures, procedures, and
so forth, are associated with everyday, practical activities

and are intended to remind us that we are feeding more than just the body. Rituals, in contrast, are more formal ceremonies intended to dramatically shift the minds and consciousness of the participants.

Informal customs, such as gracing the home with flowers, adorning it with art, and decorating it with any sort of beauty, including furnishings, serve to sanctify the space. Other customs, such as listening to music, reading, writing letters, sharing a cup of coffee, pursuing hobbies, and enjoying conversations, are all reminders that the real purpose of these activities is to nourish our spirits.

Naturally the greatest number of customs are associated with the most frequently undertaken activities. There are customs for every part of the cooking and eating process, for example. In ancient times, food was never cooked on the hearth fire. The hearth was treated with respect. Until the last couple of centuries, cooking was actually done outside or in a separate building, never in the house. Carrion in the home was considered unbefitting a sanctuary space. Some foods became acceptable and others taboo. Special foods existed for special days. Plum pudding at Christmas and Easter eggs are just two modern examples. Ordinary meals required ordinary customs or manners, such as not eating prior to the host and hostess, giving blessings or saying grace prior to eating, offering toasts at the conclusion of the meal, and so forth. Many of these cultural customs, such as the custom of "breaking bread," find their way into family traditions and become a legacy that sanctifies the activity.

There are even customs concerning cleaning. Spring cleaning, for example, was a time set aside to refresh the entire sanctuary. Chinese families traditionally do their annual cleaning just prior to Chinese New Year; Jewish families do it before Passover. Even the hearth fire had to be refreshed once a year—hence the tradition of the Yule log in England.

Whatever their superficial purpose, the real purpose of

everyday customs is to remind us of the joy and sweetness of life itself. Rituals, on the other hand, are intended to shift consciousness from everyday activities to that other quality of being, our truest self.

Rituals

Rituals, which are usually associated with overwhelming events in one's bodily life, are intended to focus attention back to the spirit of life. Unlike simple customs, rituals often have three parts: first, the former way of being is brought to a close by a concluding act or event; second, a transition period occurs, in which seclusion is often required; finally, a new period begins, when participants are ready to embrace and trust the unknown. This new beginning is often marked by a festival or celebration. These are the same three steps that mark the transformation of a caterpillar into a butterfly. Each step is indispensable to the transformation process.

In addition to formal ritual space, such as a church, many rituals take place in the home. Most common may be threshold rituals. Just as the right to decide who enters your home is protected by law, entry rites are upheld by ceremony. All threshold rites are intended to symbolize a departure from ordinary, outside consciousness in preparation for observing the peace and sanctity of the sanctuary. That's why brides are carried over it. Hats are doffed. Weapons and other evidence of fear and anger are left outside. Different clothes are often donned. Street shoes are often replaced with other footwear or slippers. Ritual gestures, similar to what one does upon entering a church or temple, are common. The language spoken may even change to that of an old country. Latin, Greek, or Hebrew is the norm in certain religious traditions. The threshold is also memorialized by physical symbol, such as Jewish mezuzahs, Christian fishes, horseshoes, garlic, hex signs, and others. Serving as a place as well as a space, thresholds are intended to ensure that no part of the outside world is brought into the sanctuary.

Less frequent, yet even more important, are rituals that mark passages in life, such as birth, death, war, initiation into adulthood, and other significant events. These are known as *purification rituals*. Returning warriors, for example, were thought to pollute the space with their anger and fear. Thus Celtic warriors were immersed in three successive tubs of water to purify them. No step could be skipped (as America learned with Vietnam veterans) if warriors were to succeed in rejoining society. Childbirth, though a supreme act of love, has rituals that conform to the same pattern. There are showers before and after the child is born, and there's often a seclusion period in between. Sadly, in the name of efficiency and economic necessity, people in contemporary life have lost the benefit of this ritual grace period. A period of seclusion and transition is also part of the ritual of death. Unfortunately, rituals concerning death are often misperceived. For example, earlier in this century a popular homemaker's magazine refused to take any articles that referred to the parlor because it reminded the editor of the place where a deceased person was laid out for viewing. Eventually the custom of viewing the dead person was transferred to the funeral parlor (now called a funeral *home*), and the parlor was renamed the "living" room. This editor obviously didn't understand how the ritual of passing one's last days, giving blessings, absolving others of guilt, and dying in dignity is an act of love. As such, rather than pollute the space as he apparently believed, it actually sanctifies it.

Rituals are more prevalent than most people realize. Unfortunately, because they often get passed down without explanation, their purpose and meaning are frequently forgotten. This problem is exacerbated by the hectic pace of the modern world. Attention shifts to outward signs, and the original beauty of the ritual is lost. It's similar to appreciating the details of the picture frame and losing sight of the painting. Form is mistaken for content. Happily, our spirit never forgets the truth. No matter how many centuries have passed, the time eventually arrives when the value of these rituals comes back into full view. This is one of those times. Failing to find the sustenance of sanctuary in the outside world, people are coming home to the experiences that sanctify their life.

Money

Money is usually associated with the fears and ambitions of the world, yet there are two sides to the coin. Money may actually be the most common, everyday means of nurturing the spirit as well as feeding the body. After all, money is not our master; it's our creation. It has no more inherent meaning than we've given it. When Jesus of Nazareth said, "Render unto Caesar that which is Caesar's and unto God that which is God's," ancient people immediately understood that money was intended to keep the home fires burning as well as pay the taxes of life. All the coins of antiquity had the spirit of life represented by divine images on one side of the coin and the practical, material world represented by the image of a ruler on the other side. People knew that money was intended to nourish the spirit of life as well as feed the body. Although in modern times we have moved this idea to the rim of the coin, the concept has not been stamped out.

Money is intended to nurture the home sanctuary as much today as it was in the time of Caesar. An especially good way to use money is on a smart, hardworking mortgage that builds equity ownership every month. Money that builds real home ownership is money wisely invested.

Security

Home is also refuge. It's shelter and protection against the elements. It's a major source of our comfort, convenience, safety, storehouse, health and welfare, entertainment, and community. The "information highway" even makes it possible to maintain a full-time career and never leave the home.

Home should be the safest place in the world. Not just because of its bricks and mortar, but also because of the social customs created to surround it with a golden circle of protection. Everything and everyone, including guests, within the circle are protected. This tradition goes back to the time of knights and chivalry when there were special places enclosed by ribbons in which the knights displayed their glamour and noble virtues. No weapons or hostile gestures were tolerated within the space. To this day special protection extends to certain places and buildings. Churches, monasteries, and embassies are places of special refuge. General Manuel Noriega of Panama took refuge in a papal embassy building, for instance, and American forces had to wait for him to come out of his own volition. So strong and so much trust is put in this golden circle of protection that when a home has been burglarized the cry is always the same: "I feel personally violated."

Indeed, when our home has been burglarized, not only has our personal refuge been violated, our spiritual sanctuary has also been penetrated. Feelings of violation can be just as great if the threat is economic, not physical. In fact, aside from random violence and urban terrorism, the most widespread threat to the home sanctuary *is* economic. Ours is an economic world. Because of that fact, the average American enjoys an unparalleled standard of living. But the economic world has unparalleled dangers too. Every time the economy undergoes a major transition, millions of people suffer. Unlike the ancient, natural world, when an individual could slay the boar threatening his family, a single person cannot prevent economic transitions from occurring. Change is eternal.

Although we cannot prevent change, we *can* prevent aspirations of personal gain and worldly ambitions from threatening the home. These ambitions start innocently enough. Typically we're motivated by a simple desire to do well for our families. But we sometimes lose our balance; instead of receiving so as to give, or rather than serving something higher than ourselves, we begin to take risks and gamble to attain personal ambitions. This phenomenon is part of the human drama. It's not a new story. Euripides told it in the ancient Greek theater, and today it's being replayed on TV soap operas. The only difference is that now we live in an economic world, where the games of ambition are played out with money. It is precisely these money games that put the home sanctuary at risk.

These gambles are seldom motivated by profit alone. Usually it's the quest for social image, creature comforts, and the apparent security of possessions that are the stronger motivations. So, rather than buying a home within the peace and comfort of our financial resources, we're tempted to buy the most expensive house possible. To afford it we burden ourselves with a lifetime of mortgage payments. As a consequence, instead of building ownership, we're resigned to simply managing debt. Instead of building a nest egg for the future, we gamble that appreciation will bail us out. Thus, instead of safeguarding the home sanctuary, we've violated our first duty and put it at risk.

These mistakes are all motivated by innocent reasons. They're understandable ones too when you consider that home appreciation has until recently been the largest single source of a homeowner's nest egg. There seems to be little other choice but to *take* these risks. Lifetime employment with a secure pension was a feature of the old industrial economy but not of the new technological one. Consequently, the temptation is to leverage the home with more debt in the hope that greater profits will make up the difference. Yet the hope of financial gain is certainly not worth the risk of losing the home. The home mustn't be a profit venture; it's sanctuary.

Instead of gambling that home appreciation will compensate for economic changes, the other and better way to safeguard the financial security of the home is to mirror the way life itself renews abundance. First, never attempt to resist change. Embrace it. Second, reduce your vulnerability to the most fierce and uncertain aspects of change. Finally, gather up your resources and get ready to employ them in a surprising new direction. Have you ever noticed the amazing way in which Mother Nature rejuvenates herself? Shortly after a fire has cleared the old timber, new shoots of life come up more abundantly than before. Indeed, moving in overall harmony with change, reducing vulnerability, and preserving resources for a fresh new beginning is the best way to safeguard the home sanctuary during economic transitions.

An excellent way to apply this overall approach is to lower encumbrances against the home, possess a smart, hardworking mortgage, and build a solid foundation of real equity ownership. Indeed, switching away from a strategy based on simply managing debt and toward a strategy designed to build real equity ownership is a rewarding step. It provides the strength and perseverance to withstand waves of economic change, along with crosscurrents and undertows. Even though the economic world is like a wolf at the door, it's only dangerous if it can get past the threshold.

Furthermore, in addition to safeguarding the peace, sanctity, and security of the home sanctuary, building equity ownership also helps us enjoy relaxation and quietude, experience our truest selves, and awaken to the joy and sweetness of life.

A Last Word

Sanctuary is such a vast subject that we've only begun to scratch the surface. We haven't even mentioned the importance of home to a child. For a child, home is the center of the entire universe. It's where he or she is connected to all the important people in the world. This may include not only parents but grandparents, aunts, uncles, cousins, and the rest of a family. It also includes friends, schoolmates, teachers, coaches, religious leaders, and all of the child's other heroes and heroines. Children also believe that home is connected with the rest of the community, nation, and world: its ripples seem to reach out and touch everything in the universe. And they are right!

If we could see a home through the eyes of a child, we might see a cloud floating in the living room floor. The Zen master Thich Nhat Hanh believed that: The cloud must be there, for without the cloud there would be no rain. Without rain to nourish the soil there would be no trees, and without trees there would be no lumber with which to build the house and its floor. The cloud is essential for the home to exist.

Seen in this context, the cloud and the home *inter-are*. They are interconnected.

If we look even deeper, we can see sunshine. Without sunshine, the trees could not grow and the home could not be. So, sunshine and the home inter-are. Looking deeper yet, we can see the lumberjack who harvested the tree for lumber. Still deeper, we can see his parents. Without the logger's parents, the home would not exist; they too are interconnected. In fact, when we look at a home, there is actually nothing that is not in it. There are sun, rain, earth, trees, loggers, parents, schools, roads, ships, manufacturing plants, food, minerals, medicine, science, government, and on and on and on. The child is indeed right: home *is* the center of the entire universe. There's even a cloud in it.

Our intellects may have forgotten this interbeing, as well as the sanctuary aspect of home, yet our hearts have always remembered: Home is sacred space.

Heading On . . .

In addition to its serious aspects, life can also be a gentle laugh. Consider fairy tales and fables, for instance. They reveal essential truths that have been learned and handed down through the centuries. One of my favorite storytellers is Aesop. By way of history, Aesop is said to have started his career as a slave in Athens in 650 B.C. His wit, wisdom, and literary skill were so great that they eventually won him his freedom. They also earned him the privilege of being thrown off a cliff (an occupational hazard for Greek philosophers), but that's another story. His fame outlasted his short life, mainly on the strength of his fables concerning insects, animals, and other creatures whose behavior sometimes appears more human than the behavior of some humans.

The particular fable I have in mind is "Hercules and Plutus."

> When Hercules was raised to the dignity of a god and took his place on Olympus, he went round and paid his respects to all the gods and goddesses, excepting only the God of Wealth, to whom he made no sign. This caused much astonishment, and Jupiter, at the first favorable opportunity, asked Hercules for an explanation. "Why," answered he, "I have seen that god in the company of such rascals when on earth that I did not know whether it would be considered reputable to be seen talking to him in heaven."

When money is used only to satisfy the demands of the body, it indeed becomes a rascal. When it's used to nourish the needs of the spirit, though, and help build the peace, sanctity, and security we deserve, it becomes a friend indeed.

In the next chapter, you shall see why building equity ownership also moves in harmony with the economic world of the 1990s and beyond.

2
Taking Ownership

Change: The Dance of Life

Life is growth, and growth is change. The idea that the fundamental purpose of change is to nourish and create greater abundance is older than most people suspect. New archaeological studies and scientific methods have determined that ancient civilizations in the fertile crescent surrounding the Mediterranean gave their greatest honor to the forces that created life, not destroyed it. It was the chalice they revered, not the sword. As Riane Eisler noted in her stunning 1987 book, *The Chalice and the Blade*, the Minoan culture, for example, abounds with symbols, such as a stylized butterfly, and other art that reflect fertility and the creative powers of the universe. Even the design of their grave sites echoed the birthing process, as they came to understand that endings were really new beginnings and that change is the way nature rejuvenates itself.

The interpretation of endings as good, not bad, is a cornerstone of all major philosophies. It is the constant theme in the tales of every culture in the world, primitive and civilized, ancient and modern. It was precisely the observation that beginnings grow out of endings that Lao-tzu had in mind when he wrote *The Way of Life* (*Tao-te Ching*) in 604 B.C. One of his more famous but tricky phrases addresses that point: "And the is is the was of what shall be." In the Old Testament, Ecclesiastes shows that life moves in cycles: generations come and go, but the earth remains the same; the sun rises in the east and sets in the west only to rise again; the rain rolls off the mountain into the ocean only to end up on top of the mountain again; and so forth. In a similar fashion the message that the old must die before rebirth is possible is implicit in the celebration of a Christian Easter. Jesus ends his life on one day, spends a dormant period in the tomb, and rises from the dead more glorious than in previous life. The theme that endings, even death, are actually the beginnings of a new and better life is woven endlessly throughout the human tapestry.

Indeed, change is eternal. Century after century it proceeds along the same pattern: an ending, a transition period, and then a beginning. Each of these three steps is essential to renewed abundance. This three-step process of change, exemplified by the transformation of a caterpillar into a butterfly, applies less obviously but just as surely to human beings. Indeed it is a metaphor that applies specifically to economic matters.

The following story chronicles the amazing 2,500-mile odyssey of monarch butterflies across America and Mexico. The natural history aspect of the story is interesting enough, but the real message is that each step in the process is indispensable to fulfilling a greater mission.

Picture yourself standing in an open field at 4:30 in the morning in upstate New York during late July. As a distant bonfire of red light begins to break over the eastern horizon, small sounds begin to fracture this most quiet time of day. Listening with the discernment of a symphony conductor, you begin to hear a small chorus of chewing sounds. The music seems to be coming from everywhere and nowhere at the same time. And so it is. As if singing praise for a new day, a mighty chorus of monarch caterpillars chews its way to new life.

Hatched from tiny eggs that look amazingly like baby white onions, and laid on the underside of milkweed leaves, the caterpillars immediately begin a frenzy of eating that lasts but two short weeks. Weighing less than a dust ball at birth, and looking like a wet strip of glue to which someone added a drop of black ink for a head, the caterpillar feeds almost incessantly on the protein-rich leaves of the milkweed plant until it increases its weight an astonishing 2,750 times. On its body you begin to distinguish black lines and a yellow tint that foreshadow its later black and gold glory. By the time it has eaten its fill and stored up enough energy, a silent command is given and the caterpillar ceases all eating. Now it attaches its tail to the underside of a milkweed leaf and peers up at it like an upside-down shrimp. The caterpillar then secretes a substance and weaves a protective cocoonlike structure that encloses its entire body. The completion of this structure marks the beginning of a transformation that will begin an epic odyssey.

The beginning of this second cycle would be frightening to all but Mother Nature's little creatures. They move in harmony with change. When it comes time to stop eating the milkweed plant, which has permeated its body with a sticky, white sap that is poisonous to all predators (a bird never eats more than one monarch butterfly in its life), the caterpillar takes heed and waits for the next process to begin.

After the caterpillar completes the cocoonlike structure, next begins the miraculous chrysalis period. Inside this green-blue sleeping bag of a structure the caterpillar assumes the quiet of a deep coma. A chrysalis doesn't really sleep, however. On the contrary, it is hard at work. The caterpillar all but dissolves into a semisolid substance, similar to a sweet potato but more the color of an avocado. Hardly anything is left of the old creature. It abandons the outdated parts of itself and creates new parts that will be

better suited to the demands of its new world. After another two weeks of tremendous activity, the old caterpillar bursts forth as a fully transformed butterfly.

A cocoon period is indispensable to virtually every transition. It would be too dangerous without one. For instance, there are innumerable ways the caterpillar could run out of energy and perish before completing its miraculous transformation. Birds might not eat it, but it's vulnerable to myriad other catastrophes: violent summer thunderstorms, for instance, or falling on the ground and being trampled. The cocoon is a caterpillar's sanctuary. Not only does it provide protection; it allows the monarch caterpillar to prepare for its role in another of Mother Nature's secret missions.

Emerging from its cocoon sanctuary, the black and orange wings of the new monarch butterfly are so thin that light shines through them as through stained-glass windows of a gothic church. The rest of its body has also been tapered to lift lightly aloft and be carried long distances. It's a good thing too, for this butterfly is now to embark on a 2,500-mile migration to the forests of central Mexico. Despite its dainty appearance, this butterfly is nonetheless a rugged creature. We see only its floating, dipping, and tasting the nectar of a fresh flower, yet this butterfly flies on southbound breezes that sometimes go over 35 miles an hour. (One tagged butterfly was reported to have traveled 265 miles in a single day.) Six weeks later it arrives at these remote mountain locations. So many millions of butterflies have come from everywhere east of the Rocky Mountains; so thick are they on the trees that they change the color of the forest from green to orange. What an impressive feat!

But why have these monarch butterflies made such an odyssey? Nothing this grand in nature is without purpose, yet mystery still surrounds it. What is their secret mission? It must be important. Why else would there be such an elaborate protection system that enables a frail creature to travel over half of the United States and Mexico? Though there is substantial evidence that their mission is to travel far afield and pollinate flowers, plants, and crops with pollen from strains of other plants many hundreds of miles away, no one knows for sure. What's clear, however, is that it's important for these butterflies to travel vast distances and pollinate the ecosystem as they go.

After arriving in Mexico they spend the next seven months in a semihibernation. There they stay and mate until it's time to start the migration back to their birthplaces. This current wave of butterflies makes it as far as the gulf states, where they lay their eggs and then die. Their offspring, though, make it all the way back to wherever their parents started, back to the exact milkweed patch in upstate New York, for instance. This generation lays its eggs in mid-July. Soon thereafter the process begins all over again as the grandchildren of the original generation race back to Mexico for the winter.

Nature may have been replaced by economics as man's primary source of abundance, yet change still follows the same pattern. First, the current economic cycle inches its way toward the end of the cycle in the same way a caterpillar moves inextricably toward the chrysalis period. Second, it enters a transition period when it may appear that nothing constructive is happening. Either it's as quiet as a cocoon, or it seems quite destructive. Finally, signs of a new beginning emerge and take wing to produce an economy that becomes more abundant than all that have gone before it.

Each century has indeed brought a higher quality of life to the common man. The average American today lives better than past kings. We have more comfortable houses, better education opportunities, superior medical care, better clothing, a constant supply of varied fruits and spices (it's hard to imagine that people actually once fought wars over spice), healthier and more delicious food, longer life expectancy, greater ability to travel and recreate, more entertainment opportunities, and a greater number of other advantages than a king of a wealthy country enjoyed or even imagined during the time of the American Revolution. This is especially amazing since there are more people alive today than have ever lived in the history of the planet. Why does the average American live better than ever? It can't be that there are more natural resources. No more exist today than existed during the time of Julius Caesar. The answer lies in human imagination and energy. We have replaced nature with an economy whose abundance is based on ideas, not the limitations of physical goods. It's the power of these ideas that has produced a higher standard of living for the common man. The forthcoming economy promises to outshine them all.

But economic changes usually bring danger as well. The pain and suffering of the Great Depression of the 1930s is only the most recent example. As for the caterpillar, it's the transition period that's most dangerous. It's the time when resources are scarce and vulnerability is greatest. It's also a time when we tend to be least flexible, precisely because the future is so unclear. Yet, and as for the caterpillar, the key to navigating past these dangerous times is not to resist change or attempt to continue in the same old fashion but to follow rules or guidelines that help move us in harmony with the process itself.

Learning how to move in harmony with economic change is especially pertinent in the 1990s as America moves out of a 45-year economy based on industrial production and defense spending in the cold war and into a new economy based on technology, information, and services. Although this new economy will eventually provide a new and higher standard of living, there are certain to be casualties during the transition period.

The Changing Economy

The old industrial economy is passing on. Its lifetime jobs, steady promotions, pay raises, secure pensions, generous benefits, prestige, and permanent citizenship in the community are now the exception, not the rule. We can't ignore these changes, nor can we stop them. We can't outsmart them either. Going on as though nothing is different is also too risky. These changes affect everything: government finances, the pension and retirement system, housing prices, financial institutions, even time-proven ways of planning for the future. Since we can't escape these changes, the next best alternative is to move through the transition period with the least amount of resistance and danger. To this end, it will be valuable to know what the economists think about the transition period. Unfortunately, few of them agree.

Indeed, they are no more agreed about the future than anyone else. Probably less so, as it is becoming more and more apparent that the economy is not like an automobile, where you can push buttons, turn wheels, shift gears, and change the spark plugs with predictable results. The economy has become so complex with so many unintended consequences, mysterious workings, and surprises, for which there is no operator's manual, that more and more economists are coming to realize it may not be "manageable." Add to this mix an economy that is half based on ideas, and it's obvious there are no levers or switches that will change the minds of 250 million Americans overnight. This psychological factor is becoming even more powerful as the economy turns away from production of goods and toward intellectual property as its core strength. Having noted all that, there are nonetheless four major schools of opinion. Three of these schools see problems ahead.

The first group contends that the economy is essentially sound and that the transition period will be relatively smooth sailing. Former president George Bush was an advocate of this theory. Then, as now, this group looks to an economy as represented by the Wall Street financial markets, especially the stock market, as well as interest rates and corporate profits as proof of a healthy economy.

Technical and statistical data, such as productivity, small business formation, job growth, housing starts, and so forth likewise indicate that we will flow into the new economy with little trouble. Dislocations caused by ballooning debt will be mitigated by government programs and regulations. A safety net of social services will ensure that any possible downturn will have a soft landing. They point to the containment of the savings and loan crisis as an example of this management. All in all, they believe there is little to worry about.

Another group, to which President Bill Clinton belongs, believes America must get back to basics before it can arrive at a healthy new economy. The longer we wait, the worse the transition period. The root of our problem, this school says, is our habit of consuming more than we produce. Equally bad is the borrowing and spending binge that goes along with it. This borrowing is effectively sucking the marrow out of the economy. Instead of being used to increase productivity, it has subsidized consumption and speculation. Millions of jobs have been lost as companies have broken up to pay the cost of the debt. The origin of this problem is as much a personal attitude as it is a financial or economic condition. As Richard D. Lamm, the former governor of Colorado, stated, ". . . our competitors build factories, while we build opulent homes. Their exports grow, while our imports increase. They emphasize responsibility when we emphasize personal rights. They invest in the future, as we mortgage ours. They save and add to their national wealth; we spend and dissipate ours." In short, they're intent on producing, while we're satisfied with consuming. The leaders of this back-to-basics school think there's still time to reverse these trends and prevent a bad hangover during the transition period. It won't be easy. We must take our medicine now, as our borrowing and spending binge won't end by itself.

The third school of thought thinks there will be a very long and dreary period marked by a steady decline in our standard of living—a veritable Chinese water torture of slow economic rot. Despite a robust Wall Street and corporate economy, this group looks to the average pocketbook for "proof of the pudding." Proponents of this theory note that the cost of essential items that make up the quality of life has risen dramatically, while income has failed to keep pace. The net result is that our quality of life worsens with each passing year. As irrefutable evidence that the quality of life and the size of the middle class is diminishing every year, they point to the decline of affordable housing, the scant possibility of home ownership for young people, the exorbitant cost of health insurance and medical care, greater taxation, the inaccessibility of higher education for all but the privileged, blighted cities and crumbling facilities, ghetto hellholes, gangs, drugs, crime and violence, homelessness, shrinking employment opportunities, loss of job security, disappearing pensions, and other conditions, which were enumerated in *America, What Went Wrong*, by Pulitzer Prize winners Donald Barlett and James Steele. Without substantial changes in the tax system, the federal deficit, government spending, pension plans, etc., this group believes, the transition period is bound to be severe.

The fourth school, a renegade from the mainstream schools, comes in and out of vogue. It expects a savage recession or an actual depression similar to that of the 1930s. It notes that no economy in the past has survived a major collapse in the savings and loan industry, massive real estate losses, the failure of major corporations, layoffs of 40,000 workers at a time, federal deficits reaching the point of no return, and similar failures and not gone into a depression. It furthermore looks on the inability of government to work effectively, the decay of major cities, the alienation of the population, drugs, violence, and crime and concludes that things are getting worse, not better. It believes a good watershed is necessary to cleanse the system of its excesses. It's astonished it hasn't happened yet. Perhaps it hasn't happened because of new factors in a "world economy." Perhaps the strength of our trading partners in the rest of the world offsets weakness in the American economy. No one knows. As a matter of fact, it's precisely because no one can explain why the economy is staying afloat that the *"Titanic"* school thinks it must come tumbling down.

Each of these four schools presents such a plausible case that it's exceedingly difficult to prove which is an accurate prediction about the transition period. Every piece of evidence presented seems valid. No school can prove another school wrong. Yet they can't all be right. Perhaps none is correct. Perhaps each opinion is based more on personal preference and political philosophy than on solid economic proof. About the only point on which economists agree is that America is overspent and underinvested. Otherwise, they're prepared to be once again surprised by the imaginative twists and turns the economy typically uses to reinvent itself. In other words, economists don't know.

In the absence of knowing whether the transition period will be savage, but knowing that things may be very different indeed, it would be wise to nurture yourself by taking extra precautions to protect the sanctuary against an economic maelstrom. In addition to not overextending yourself, it might be wiser yet to go into a financial cocoon until you're confident that the personal finance strategy that worked for the past 25 years will continue to work for the next 25 years. This is a timely issue, because there is strong evidence that the major ways prosperity filtered down to the average American, such as secure pensions and home appreciation, are undergoing significant change and won't provide the kind of security and nest egg you expect. Presuming this is even remotely true, you must take responsibility for providing your own financial security and peace of mind.

Taking Charge

Taking charge is such an old-fashioned idea that it reminds me of a fairy tale. I like fairy tales because they get right to the heart of the matter. They communicate essential truths. Ultimately they're a gentle reminder that life isn't your master; it's your child.

The tale I have in mind is "The Three Little Pigs," a story about personal responsibility. More specifically, it's about accepting reality and ensuring the safety of your home sanctuary by building a solid foundation. You aren't counting on others or good luck to keep the wolf away from the door. You're prepared to provide it yourself.

So simple, so wise.

The following is a condensed and edited rendition of the 1892 *Green Fairy Book* adventures of Blacky, Browny, and Whitey, otherwise known as the Three Little Pigs.

> Now there came a time when the mother pig felt she needed to build a house for each of her children. "Now, Browny, what sort of house would you like to have?" "A house of mud, so I can relax and enjoy myself all day," replied Browny. "And you, Whitey?" said the mother pig in a rather sad voice. "A house of cabbage, so I can eat whenever I want," answered Whitey. "Foolish, foolish child," said the mother pig. "And you, Blacky?" "A house of brick, please, Mother, as it will be warm in the winter and cool in the summer and safe all year around." "That's a sensible little pig," replied his mother. "And now there's one last piece of advice. When our old enemy the wolf hears that I am gone, he is sure to try to get hold of you. He is very sly and will no doubt disguise himself and pretend to be a friend. Don't let him in your house on any pretext whatever."

Sure enough, Browny and Whitey believed in one pretext or another and were completely vulnerable when the wolf huffed and puffed and blew their houses of mud and cabbage apart. Blacky, who was the smartest and best-looking pig (so they say), saved his brother and sister by taking the responsibility for building a solid home and trusting only the hair on his chinny-chin-chin.

Taking personal responsibility is the key to weathering the transition period and emerging in the new economy with the strength and resources to take advantage of new opportunities. No longer can you rely on the prosperity of outside forces or others to do it for you. The tactics that worked for the parents and grandparents of the baby boom generation probably won't work for them. Social Security will soon be a shadow of its former self, so you can't rely on that system either. Even home appreciation will probably do little better than keep pace with inflation. Forewarned of these changes, you're empowered to take certain steps that will prevent them from harming you. If they don't come to pass as indications appear, you've gained an insurance policy and an opportunity for a double win. You can't lose!

In Our Parents' Footsteps

Like generals who prepare for the next engagement according to the lessons of the last war, we too follow the successful strategy of our parents and grandparents. The lessons we learn sitting on a parent's knee last a lifetime.

It may surprise you to learn that the current generation of retirees is one of the wealthiest groups in America. They enjoyed the greatest prosperity in history (and some of its biggest bumps). Houses they bought for $5,000 were sold for $150,000. They may be collecting three pensions, including a Social Security check that increases every year. Furthermore, as members of the Depression generation, most of them have been lifelong savers and also have nest eggs of their own. Understandably, they encourage us to emulate their way of building a nest egg. With such a success record, we're inclined to want to follow in their footsteps. Unfortunately, the circumstances that surrounded their success no longer prevail. Conditions appear to be just the opposite for their baby boom offspring.

Specifically, real income for the Depression generation rose steadily between 1945 and 1975. In contrast, for the baby boom generation real income has been stagnant since 1975. *Real income* means net income, after inflation and other aberrations have been factored out. Similarly, the cost of financing capital purchases, notably homes, stayed relatively low for the Depression generation. For instance, the actual interest "expense" of their mortgage was less than their interest "rate." Contemporary home buyers, on the other hand, pay more interest expense than their interest rate. (Don't worry, this is fully explained in the next chapter.) The net result is that baby boomers are paying 6 times more to buy their homes than their parents or grandparents did. This is but one example of substantially lower costs for the currently retired generation. Other essential costs, such as health, life, disability, car, and home insurance; education; transportation; local taxes; and so forth, were also substantially lower. Ironically, the things that were luxuries to our parents, such as wristwatches, are now inexpensive. Essentials, such as a pair of well-made, sturdy shoes, are now priced as luxuries. Indeed, time and real prosperity in the post–World War II economy increased the spread between what our parents owned and what they owed. Add soaring home appreciation, which was due in no small part to a huge baby boomer generation bidding up prices, and you can see how our parents and grandparents became a happy bunch of retirees.

Alas, the sons and daughters of "Rosie the Riveter" may have become biotechnicians, space scientists, financiers, advertising gurus, personal injury attorneys, or attained other glamorous careers, but they cannot assume that time is their friend. Not only is home appreciation less than a sure thing, jobs aren't secure. Income doesn't rise steadily. Pension plans aren't like money in the bank. Essential costs don't allow for a single breadwinner in the family. A host of other factors make the economy of the baby boomers not the economy of their parents and grandparents. In the face of such reality we cannot rely on outdated techniques to build a nest egg for us. We have to take charge ourselves.

The Retirement System

The problem with the science of forecasting is predicting the future. My intention in this section isn't so much to predict the future of the retirement system as it is to note the reasons it won't be like that of the past.

There are three reasons the retirement system of today will not be the retirement system of tomorrow:

1. Baby boomers will need more money than any group before them. They are the largest generation in history. They will be retiring younger and living longer than previous generations.
2. The smaller baby bust generation won't be able to support even the current level of benefits for the baby boomers.
3. The capital needed to make up the shortfall doesn't exist. The money has already been spent.

Seventy-five million babies were born in this country between 1946 and 1964, making this the largest generation in history. It's similar to a pyramid with the largest group at the base. Thus, despite there being no money in Social Security, the sheer size of this group has been able to fund the benefits of current retirees. Unfortunately, the baby boomers will not reap the same benefits once they retire.

Supposedly, their benefits will be paid by workers who are just now coming into the system. But there won't be enough workers to go around. The pyramid will have turned upside down, with the smallest group at the bottom.

Not only is this generation much smaller, but its income will be smaller as well. The corporate ethic is to retain as few employees as possible, thus reducing the size of contributions even further. Power and prestige now go to companies with the fewest employees, not those that employ the most. Wall Street rewards them every time they slash their payroll. This trend promises to continue as these companies move operations offshore to employ cheaper workers. These trends, as well as demographic changes, cannot be reversed. To maintain today's standard of benefits in the year 2025, it's estimated that workers would have to pay 40 percent of their income in Social Security taxes. You must not assume this will be allowed to happen. Is *hara-kiri* too strong a term?

Adding to the problem is that baby boomers will live longer than their predecessors. Four times as many people now live past age 65 as in 1950. By the year 2025, eight times as many people will live past age 65 as did in 1950. This means that one of every two people will live past age 65 and will need financial support. Adding to the cost of baby boom retirement is the specialized medical care required by such an aging population. Furthermore, forced and early retirement is adding to the length of the retirement period. It's estimated that baby boomers may have 20 to 30 years of retirement. The amount of money needed to enjoy 20 years of golden retirement is quite substantial.

Unfortunately, most pension plans, including Social Security, are woefully underfunded. Private employer pension plans are far less secure than most people think. Many of us think that once money is put into a retirement fund it stays there until withdrawn by the beneficiary. Wrong! The law allows company owners to withdraw money under a number of permissive guidelines. This has enabled companies to use this money to stave off hard times and leave little or nothing if they go bankrupt. It's also given corporate raiders an opportunity to write themselves a free check to be used on whatever they like. Buy another company, perhaps?

Medical pension plans aren't much better. They're terribly underfunded. Employers have banked on using then-current revenue to fund future commitments. This sounds good until the tab is added up—it's so large it threatens to bankrupt some of our largest corporations. No wonder they're trying to wriggle out of it. It's easy to be critical of these corporate managers, but they're just following the example of Uncle Sam.

Social Security is broke. Contrary to the claim of a surplus, which politicians are fond of mentioning, the fund doesn't have any real money. Unlike independent private pension plans, the money isn't in any bank, invested in blue-chip securities, or in sound real estate. It's all been spent to reduce the annual budget deficit. In fact, it's counted twice: once in the Social Security fund and again in reporting a lower budget deficit amount. The government gives Social Security a paper IOU, but the government has no ability to repay it. It is so far in the hole already, and the politicians are so loath to raise a sufficient amount of taxes or reduce spending, that it'll never be repaid. What's the solution? There will be no alternative but to cut benefits.

By the time baby boomers reach retirement age, the current retirement system will be only a shadow of its former self. It won't be gone altogether—I believe the will of the American people is too strong to tolerate that. And politicians do want to be reelected. Yet benefits will have to be altered radically. The eventual outcome is anyone's guess. Those banking on Social Security, however, face the prospect of becoming a tragic statistic. Your job is to make sure you're not one of them.

Taking personal responsibility for building your own nest egg is the key to weathering this storm.

Coffee Break

Coffee breaks are an opportunity to get up, stretch your legs, and reflect on the many reasons that *Future Shock* is now. We've covered a lot of topics, ranging from the secret mission of monarch butterflies to ancient acknowledgment of the three-step process of change, the changing economy, taking charge and the Three Little Pigs, and, last, the retirement system. The purpose of this break is to let all that information sink in before moving on to related matters.

I like to take a walk and visit my favorite coffee shop, which is named after the first mate in the novel *Moby Dick*. And my break wouldn't be complete without visiting Barbara at the Blue Point bakery for a delicious slice of peach-blueberry pie. I usually take a pencil and a little notebook too, because it won't be long before connections between my personal situation and the material start popping into my mind. As much as I like to believe that I'll remember all my ideas, I know it won't be 10 minutes before I can't recall half of them. My notebook captures these ideas and gives me the opportunity to sort them out later.

As part of these breaks, which will appear throughout the book, I'll also provide a little exercise pertaining to recently discussed topics. The first exercise concerns arriving at a ballpark figure for the amount of money needed to maintain your lifestyle for 20 years after retirement. Many considerations such as taxes, lifestyle changes, inflation, time value of interest earnings, extraordinary expenses, college tuition, and so forth aren't included. Yet retirement planners generally agree that you'll need a surprising average of 75 percent of your former income to sustain your preretirement lifestyle. This exercise should put you in the right ballpark.

Current Income	_____
Constant Factor	___×.75_____
Annual Requirement	_____
Years in Retirement	___× 20_____
Total	_____
Pension Plans	___×.50_____
Nest Egg	_____

For example, if you earned $32,000 a year, you would need $24,000 of revenue per year to maintain your current lifestyle. Twenty years of retirement would require $480,000 of revenue. Assuming various pension plans contribute half of that amount, you will need a nest egg of $240,000 to feel financially secure.

Impressed? You should be. This is a substantial amount of money. Don't panic, though. I know you're worried that you don't earn enough revenue but as you shall see in the next chapter, you indeed already earn enough to amass the needed nest egg.

Feel free to move the numbers around. You may wish to project a higher income at the time of retirement rather than your current income. Perhaps you'd like to include a fudge factor for world travel or other dreams. Perhaps you want to use a lower percentage for pension plans (not higher). I wouldn't recommend lowering the constant factor, though, because most financial planners agree that 75 percent of former income is surprisingly accurate.

There's no need to hurry this exercise. Take as much time as you need, sleep on it overnight if you wish, and go on to the next section tomorrow.

End of Break

Home Appreciation

In lieu of building real equity ownership, the temptation is to hope that appreciation will be high enough to provide the surplus needed for a nest egg. Alas, there's strong evidence that appreciation will do little more than preserve the buying power of your capital. It almost certainly will not be high enough to provide the surplus capital on which you can lead a comfortable life.

Of course real estate will always appreciate. The question is: how much? It's not surprising that the high appreciation of the last 20 years or so has led many people to bank on its indefinite continuation. After all, it did help them obtain more money through equity appreciation than they could even imagine earning from their jobs. Unfortunately, the primary forces behind this appreciation have reversed direction. First, debt is no longer profitable. Interest expense is now and promises to remain larger than appreciation. Second, the high demand for houses that once caused the long wave of appreciation has receded in most of the country. There's now enough supply to satisfy the smaller demand of the baby bust generation. Both of these factors have changed the game in home appreciation.

Debt Is No Longer Profitable

You can no longer borrow yourself rich! Once upon a time, the opposite was true: you could borrow money at interest rates that were substantially below the rate of inflation, making debt profitable. For example, if you bought a house and paid $9,000 in annual interest expense, but inflation was high and appreciation increased the value of your house by $15,000, you made a nifty $6,000 gross profit for being in debt. Tax deductions on the interest expense increased your profit even more. Speculation pushed the appreciation rate still higher as everyone tried to climb aboard the bandwagon. The more debt, the higher the profit.

Why won't that also be the case in the future? In the past, political considerations and economic philosophy were responsible for holding interest rates below the general inflation rate. This artificial situation caused spiraling inflation and such speculation that the Federal Reserve Board finally decided to put interest rates back into proper alignment with the general inflation rate, which is normally 2 to 3 percent above inflation. To accomplish this mission the prime interest rate was hiked to 21 percent. As noted in "The Changing Economy," there are no levers or buttons that can automatically control the economy. So this particular action took six to eight years to be felt throughout the real estate market. Nonetheless, its effect was inevitable. Speculation was cut to the quick. Inflation began to notch down with each year until it hit 2–3 percent. Appreciation followed. Yet the cost of interest expense on a mortgage stayed at its original level. The homeowner who was previously making a $6,000 profit found himself with a $9,000 cash cost of interest (prior to tax deductions) for owning the property. This is a turnabout of $15,000—a devastating event for people relying on the management of debt for their next egg.

Interest rates are allowed to slip below the inflation rate only every 50 years or so. It takes about that long for banks and mortgage lenders to forget the repercussions of such an artificial situation. So many banks and S&Ls went under and careers were ruined during the last go-around that they've relearned their lesson and won't allow it to happen again in this lifetime. They're determined to keep interest rates well above the inflation rate. Even the so-called low mortgage interest rates of 1993 were 5 percent or so higher than the inflation rate. The spread on other lending rates is even higher. In fact this spread is the highest in 50 years. The era of free debt is indeed over.

Some people believe that high inflation will inevitably return, again making their debt profitable. They would do well to remember one of Aesop's fables, "The Frogs Desiring for a King." In brief, all the frogs in the kingdom complained to the god that they didn't like the big, fat frog they were given as a king. Not only wasn't he an imposing figure; they could even sit on top of him if they liked. So, according to their specifications, the god gave them a new all-powerful king—one with long legs, feathers, and a big beak, who was called "stork." The stork swallowed them, one by one, without mercy. "They lost no time in beseeching the god to give them again their former state. 'No, no,' replied he; 'a King that did you no harm did not please you. Make the best of the one you have, or you may chance to get a worse in his place.' "

In the case of inflation, if it did come roaring back, it would have an effect opposite of what most people would anticipate. This time an inflation rate of 12 percent would mean interest rates of 18 percent, for instance. Although the exact effect on real estate values would be difficult to predict, it is not difficult to understand why the effect would not be good. It would probably be the worst of both worlds.

Supply Has Caught Up to Demand

You can't count on high demand to push home appreciation up either. In fact the trend is moving in the opposite direction. The baby bust generation is significantly smaller than the baby boom generation. Their income is noticeably less. And they aren't as confident or as willing to take risks as their baby boom predecessors were. Despite local fluctuations, these demographic shifts will undoubtedly limit the amount of home appreciation.

When baby boomers came into their prime buying years, there weren't enough houses to satisfy their demand. Not only were they the largest group of home buyers in history, but older homeowners were keeping their houses longer because indexed pension plans enabled them to do so, which is an example of the law of unintended consequences. Migration to growth states added even more demand for scarce housing. The boomers were buying houses as fast as they could build them, as well as condominiums, which were being converted from apartments. Naturally, prices were bid higher and higher as the competition increased.

This is no longer the situation. There are fewer buyers—far fewer—in this wave of baby bust buyers. New household formations in the 1990s, for example, are predicted to be 34 percent lower than in the 1970s. This means there will be 6 million fewer households. It also means there will be one-third fewer buyers looking for a house. Who then is going to bid up the price on all these homes?

Compounding the effect of fewer buyers, the baby bust generation earns less money than its predecessors. As a matter of fact, its real income didn't grow at all between 1980 and 1988. It's actually 28 percent below what it was for the baby boom generation at the same age. Translated into practical terms, this means they aren't able to keep up with the appreciating price of houses. For example, a typical thirty-year-old needed only 14 percent of before-tax earnings in the 1950s to make mortgage payments on a typical house. By 1973 the percentage had risen to 21 percent. In the mid-1980s it took a whopping 44 percent of income to make mortgage payments on a median-priced house. (For many, the *GI* in *GI Financing* came to mean "Good In-Laws.") Furthermore, the additional income provided by the fresh wave of working women, which subsidized higher home prices, has been fully absorbed by prices. This source of income has stopped expanding. The combination of less income and fewer buyers contributes strong evidence against continued high appreciation.

Consumer confidence is yet another mark against high appreciation. Most buyers aren't confident of job security, let alone constant pay increases. They realize corporate America is cutting jobs to the bone. Understandably, they're less willing to go out on a limb and buy the biggest and most expensive house possible. Moreover, having seen appreciation and resale prices fall in most of the country, current buyers are very wary of appreciation's fickle nature. They realize it comes and goes outside anyone's control. Even when all the economic factors seem to be in place, such as high-tech industry, in-state migration, housing shortages, a diversified economy, and a strong employment base, appreciation and home prices can still take a nosedive as they did in Boston, New York City, and California. People thought these areas were different from the rest of the country. Many times they had said, "It can't happen here. You don't understand. This is. . . ." But it did happen, and current buyers took note. They are no longer willing to bet the ranch on appreciation.

The tide has indeed changed in home appreciation. There aren't as many buyers, they have less money and fewer career opportunities than their baby boom predecessors, and consumer confidence is lower than it once was. Thus it's not reasonable to expect that demand will push prices much above the general inflation rate. Add the end of profitable debt to low demand, and it's clear that home appreciation may preserve buying power of the capital but little more. It's certainly not a guaranteed source of money needed for your cash nest egg.

So it has come to pass that many of the major assumptions that were the foundation of our personal financial strategy have undergone profound change. Home appreciation cannot be relied on, nor can the current retirement system. Neither can we lock down our costs and let time raise everyone's boat when the economic lake goes up, as it did for our parents and grandparents. On the contrary, we must take personal responsibility and seek a more reliable way to ensure our future abundance.

Abundance Rules

Significant changes in our most cherished institutions are bound to be met with some resistance. It's human nature to resist endings, especially when the future is so unclear. One temptation is to continue on the same path, except to try to do so in a different and better fashion. We delude ourselves into thinking we can outsmart the system using better judgment and sound decisions.

Do not take this path. It's a trap. The essence of wisdom lies not in exercising better judgment but in learning to relinquish it. There's a celebrated Buddhist story that illustrates this point:

There was a farmer whose stallion ran away. His neighbors came over and said, "What terrible luck. How horrible for you." Whereupon the farmer replied, "Bad luck, good luck; who knows?" Sometime later his stallion returned with eight mares following him. His neighbors came over and said, "What great luck. You must celebrate immediately." The farmer shook his head and said, "Good luck, bad luck; who knows?" In the process of breaking in the new horses the farmer's son broke his leg. The farmer's neighbors came over and predictably said, "What a bad turn of events. Now your son can't help you in the fields, and you may go hungry this winter." To which the farmer replied, "Bad luck, good luck; who knows?" Shortly thereafter the Chinese Army came to conscript young men for one of its ceaseless wars and passed the son by because of his broken leg. Again the farmer's neighbors came over to congratulate him on his good luck, to which he again replied, "Good luck, bad luck; who knows?" Indeed, relinquishing the idea that you can judge what everything means and outsmart the wave of changes engulfing the economy will save you heartache later.

Happily, there is another way to manage the process of change and pick your way through the maze of conflicting information about the transition period. You needn't understand how, when, where, or why things are happening to be successful. All you need do is follow the rules of abundance and learn how to apply them to your personal situation.

The word *abundance* has a distinct flavor: it implies having enough to enjoy a happy life with financial security and peace of mind. This is different from *rich, wealthy,* or even *affluent,* which implies a quantity of material possessions. *Abundance,* on the other hand, speaks to the quality of life. It's because they help improve the quality of life that these rules were so named.

There are three Abundance Rules. Each rule is patterned after the three-step process of change. Each is designed to make sure you don't get caught moving in the wrong direction at the wrong time.

Rule 1. Move in harmony with change. Don't attempt to fight or ignore it.
Rule 2. Reduce your vulnerability during uncertain transition times.
Rule 3. Position yourself for new choices and opportunities.

The first rule requires that we go back to the four

schools of economic thought and note one point of agreement—individual Americans, as well as businesses, can no longer borrow their way to prosperity. It's apparent to anyone reading the daily newspaper that the tide no longer favors a debt strategy. Quite the opposite. It's penalizing them. It doesn't matter whether it's a major corporation, such as an airline, a small business, an individual, or a country. Virtually all business failures, including the collapse of insurance companies and lending institutions, real estate foreclosures, and personal bankruptcies have one thing in common—heavy debt. All tried to continue managing debt as a profitable strategy. It worked in the 1970s and part of the 1980s, but it doesn't work now.

Rule 1, which is to move in harmony with change and not attempt to fight or ignore it, may be applied by recognizing that the tide has moved against the management of debt as a profitable way to build financial security and peace of mind. All the factors that made managing debt a successful strategy have changed and gone away. And they will not return in the foreseeable future. Therefore, how Rule 1 should be applied is somewhat obvious:

Action Step 1. Stop managing debt as your primary financial strategy. The application of Rule 1 doesn't mean that all debt is bad or that you should be debt-free. That's impractical. It's also virtually impossible. It does mean, however, that you should recognize and accept the fact that pursuing a financial strategy based on managing debt is simply swimming against the tide.

Action Step 2. Avoid unnecessary interest expense. Rule 2, to reduce your vulnerability, can also be applied to the end of profitable debt. If it is no longer profitable to manage debt, interest expense is a waste of precious cash. Remember, it's the transition period that is the most dangerous. The risk is running out of precious resources before the prosperity of the new economy begins to appear.

As with debt, however, not all interest expense is bad.

The accent in Action Step 2 is on the word *unnecessary*. In this context it means interest expense paid on debt that is doing little more than supporting the outstanding balance, not buying real ownership. No doubt some people will continue to manage debt and pay exorbitant amounts of interest expense in the hope that outside forces will bail them out. This is a desperate attempt to employ old rules in a new game. It won't work.

Reducing your vulnerability by avoiding unnecessary interest expense is akin to building a safe cocoon. Instead of running out of energy and falling victim to the economic transition, a cocoon allows you to get out of harm's way. It may seem that nothing is happening during the cocoon period, but that's a false assumption. It's actually a period of tremendous transformation. The old, of whatever sort, slowly evolves until a new entity is ready to burst forth. Hence cocooning is not only a way to reduce your vulnerability; it's also an essential part of the rejuvenation process as well.

Action Step 3. Build equity ownership and a cash nest egg. Rule 3 is to position yourself for new choices and opportunities. The natural outcome of the cocoon stage is the evolution of a form that's in harmony with the new operating environment. This new form is also shaped to take advantage of new opportunities. When the caterpillar took the risk to change its former shape, it became a butterfly that now has wings and a tapered body, enabling it to travel long distances and take advantage of these new choices and opportunities. The Chinese recognize that opportunity is greatest when the situation appears to be the worst by expressing the word *crisis* with two characters, one part standing for "risk" and the other for "opportunity."

We needn't go far in our own history to prove that the prosperity of the last 45 years actually started in the depths of the Great Depression. It was a period when household appliances, such as washers, refrigerators, stoves, mixers, toasters, radios, and others found their way into the average home. The quality and production of automobiles skyrocketed. Skyscrapers penetrated heights theretofore impossible to reach. Artificial fibers such as nylon and rayon were invented. Precision instruments and airplane technology were developed during the 1930s. Much of rural America was electrified. Unparalleled construction projects such as the Golden Gate Bridge and Hoover Dam were begun. In fact, what appears to have been the worst time in economic history was actually a time when people were hard at work turning crisis into opportunity.

To take advantage of the opportunities that start to appear during the transition period, it's necessary to apply Rule 3 by switching to a personal strategy designed to build real equity ownership of your important assets, especially your home. In addition to being secure from the dangers of the transition period, those who have equity ownership and cash have the resources to take advantage of bargains, investments, and new opportunities presented by emerging technologies of the new economy.

Again, building equity doesn't mean a complete ban on debt. It does, however, mean changing the character of your borrowing from lazy debt to "smart debt." Borrowed money is smart, hardworking debt when a substantial portion of the monthly payment goes toward building real equity ownership. (Exactly when it stops being lazy debt and starts becoming smart debt is fully discussed in the next chapter.) Another criterion is repayment of the debt in the shortest possible time. As you will see in later chapters, saving time is as important as saving money. Perhaps more so. Finally, it's smart debt if it consumes the lowest possible amount of interest expense, which resonates with Action Step 2. I once read a book titled *Safe Methods of Business*, published primarily for farmers in 1886. It contended that the annual interest rate didn't necessarily represent the true cost of a loan and that the true cost could be seen only by the actual amount of cash paid on interest expense. If it required $100 of interest expense to repay a $200 loan, for example, then the true cost was 50 percent, irrespective of the stated interest rate.

All things considered, transforming your passive debt into an active investment that builds real equity ownership is the best application of Rule 3.

Each of these three steps is a powerful, practical tool to help you through the transition period, and all are easier to apply than they first appear. At first there seems to be so much momentum behind continuing obligations of the debt strategy that it will take a long time to slow down and turn it in the other direction. It seems especially hard to believe that you can build equity ownership and a nest egg of your own. After all, most people can't substantially increase their income. Furthermore, it's ridiculous to think we can trim expenses enough to amass the kind of nest egg needed to enjoy a golden future. What's the alternative? For most of us, the answer lies in the way we buy, finance, and pay off the mortgage on our home.

As our largest investment and biggest expense, the home almost invariably provides the best vehicle for implementing the action steps of an abundance strategy. The rewards for shifting to a strategy based on building equity and preserving cash come in three stages. The first stage empowers your monthly mortgage payment to purchase real equity ownership. Instead of it being wasted on unnecessary interest expense, it goes directly to principal. The second stage of rewards comes when you own your home sooner. Money previously earmarked for mortgage payments is now free to be used for such things as a cash nest egg, investments, tuition, vacations, or whatever. The third stage is earnings and income on that liberated capital. The combined effect of these three stages is far bigger than most people realize. As you shall see in the next chapter, it can amount to a $230,000 nest egg for a family earning no more than $40,000 a year. Even if it all doesn't end up in a cash nest egg, it still has the same economic value as if it did. If, for instance, $50,000 of college tuition is funded by this money instead of by borrowed funds, the economic value is the same as if it were in a nest egg. No matter the form, owning equity is better than paying interest expense.

The first task in this process is learning to look at a home mortgage from the perspective of equity rather than debt. The next chapter, "Home Economics," shows you how to make informed decisions in selecting a home mortgage. Supplementing standard mortgage criteria, which typically reflect a debt management philosophy, this chapter shows you how to evaluate your choices from an equity-wise perspective. These insights are sure to surprise you.

A Last Word and Heading On . . .

Aesop's fables were written in an era when limited natural and material resources formed the entire economy of man and unavoidable consequences befell the person who failed to take prescribed action. His fables were understandably harsh and left little wiggling room. Take "The Ant and Grasshopper," for instance. In brief, when the grasshopper was hungry in the winter, he went to the ant and asked for food. The ant asked him what he had done all summer while the ant was storing food. When the grasshopper said, "Why, all day long and all night too, I sang if you please," the ant replied, "Oh, you sang, did you? Now, then, you can dance."

Happily, we live in a different era, a time when information, technology, and intellectual property transform limited natural and material resources a thousandfold. Previous choices don't limit our future opportunities; we can change our mind and thus change our results.

The point of the next chapter is just that—to provide an opportunity to change your mind about the purpose of your home mortgage and thus transform it a thousandfold.

3
Home Economics

When we think of home economics, we typically think of high school and chocolate cakes. Yet *economy* is actually the ancient Greek word for the management of household finances. It's only appropriate that "Home Economics" be the title of a chapter devoted to helping readers make an informed decision on the selection of a home mortgage. Not only will this chapter provide unique insights to help you select an equity-wise mortgage; it will also reveal a number of secrets to help you transform an existing mortgage into smart, hardworking debt.

The Debt Perspective

There are two sides to the mortgage coin. The most familiar side is selecting a mortgage on the basis of managing debt. The standard criteria for this perspective involve the annual interest rate, monthly payment, points and fees, down payment, repayment terms, fixed versus adjustable interest rates, and so forth. The aim of this perspective usually is to get the lowest monthly "cost." It believes the purpose of the monthly payment is to support the largest possible loan balance, not to purchase equity ownership.

Likewise for the interest rate. It doesn't refer to principal or equity at all. It actually expresses an arithmetic relationship between the outstanding *loan balance* and the amount of annual interest to be paid on it. It's assumed that the lower the monthly payment, the better the mortgage.

There are several good reasons why the debt perspective dominated the mortgage landscape for the last 20 years. Foremost was affordability. Incomes had not kept up with the price of housing. Consequently, and as a practical matter, the monthly payment had to be pushed to the lowest possible amount so that buyers could qualify for a mortgage. Another reason was inflation. So long as the inflation rate was higher than the interest rate, the real cost of the mortgage appeared to be zero. The final and perhaps most attractive reason for minimizing the monthly payment was appreciation. The less paid in mortgage payments, the higher possible profit margin on an eventual sale. Taking all three reasons together, it's easy to see why managing debt was considered the best way to manage our financial affairs.

All three considerations still play a role in the average home buyer's selection of a mortgage. It's still a challenge to qualify for a mortgage loan. Lower interest rates make it appear that mortgages are cheaper than they've been for 20 years. And appreciation is still the secret hope of every homeowner. These considerations are also touted by real estate agents, financial planners, and especially lenders. After all, lenders are tied to interest rates and account for them on an annual basis. Additionally, a number of old adages and rules of thumb, such as "borrow dear and repay cheap," validate the debt perspective as being how "smart money" manages its affairs. A number of superb books on the market can tell you how to orchestrate these affairs and obtain the lowest mortgage payment.

What's not available are books that tell you how to evaluate a prospective mortgage from the equity perspective. Teaching you how to do so is the goal of this chapter.

The Equity Perspective

Selecting an equity-wise mortgage is the other side of the coin. So few people ever see this side of a mortgage, in fact, that the terminology is foreign. Yet this approach is rapidly becoming more valued than the other. And with good reason: Chapter 2 showed how important building equity is for the baby boom generation and that the greatest opportunity to build equity is to select an equity-wise mortgage.

There are three primary criteria for selecting a mortgage on the basis of its ability to build equity: purchasing power, interest expense, and initial gain/opportunity loss. In brief, *purchasing power* measures the monthly payment's contribution to principal/equity; the more, the better. Instead of desiring the lowest monthly payment, the aim is for the *largest* possible amount of payment going toward principal reduction. *Interest expense* measures the total amount of *cash* spent on interest per $1 of principal. Interest expense represents the true cost of buying equity ownership. *Initial gain/opportunity loss* considers the full hard-dollar cost or trade-off for increasing the long-term borrowing power of the monthly payment. Most people are astonished at the size of this trade-off. These simple yet powerful criteria shed an entirely new light on the process of selecting a mortgage.

When a mortgage is viewed from an equity perspective, most people are surprised to discover that the repayment schedule is a constantly changing arithmetic equation, not the flat and static one implied by the constant interest rate and constant monthly payment. Hence no single point will yield a complete measurement for each criterion. Rather, each criterion is measured at a number of points along the repayment schedule. A 30-year mortgage will have six measuring points, for instance, and a 15-year mortgage will have three.

In an effort to grade the merits of a prospective mortgage, various sections of the repayment schedule will be coded to denote their relative contribution to equity ownership. Those points deemed to contribute to equity are known in the banking industry as "blue zones." Blue zones are smart, hardworking debt. Those portions of the mortgage nearing the blue zone but still not contributing are known as "pink zones." Pink zones are still overweight with interest expense, which is a burden on the monthly payment's ability to build equity ownership. Finally, those points in the repayment schedule that contribute virtually nothing to equity and are dedicated to little more than managing debt are known as "red zones." Red zones are fat, lazy debt. The objective is to be as near to or have as many blue zones as possible.

Unfortunately, we seldom have the freedom and luxury to choose a 100 percent equity-wise mortgage. More often than not, we must consider our financial limitations along with our equity ambitions.

Selecting an Equity-Wise Mortgage

This section provides the insights and tools you need to evaluate prospective mortgages and select one based on sound information and a full understanding of all the trade-offs between the debt and equity perspectives. In addition to quantitative methods that provide pinpoint measurements of the various criteria, you will also learn how to evaluate the relative merits of each prospective mortgage. As you will soon discover, there is not a single criterion or point of measurement that tells the complete story. Nor are all the equity criteria of equal weight. That's why the blue, pink, and red zones will start at different points in the repayment schedule. This is where you come into the picture. Your job is to assess the relative merits of each prospective mortgage and determine which one is best for your personal situation.

Arlene and Don Clifton

Now is an excellent time to introduce you to Don and Arlene Clifton, a couple whose mortgage we'll use as a case study for the remainder of the book. Don and Arlene live in an Iowa college town. They're both 40-something. Their town is a nice place to live and raise a family, the kind of town Charles Kuralt would have liked to visit on his "Sunday Morning" television program. There's little excitement aside from college football games and even less crime. Not many strike it rich in this town, but fewer yet go wanting for good friends. A whirlwind of land speculation hit the farm country a few years back but subsequently left on the next good wind. Most people have now returned to the certainty of raising corn. Not many people come looking for that baseball field anymore, although quite a few are now looking for covered bridges, which is a mystery to most people around these parts. Don pursues a life insurance career. Arlene stays at home, operates a part-time telephone answering service, and cares for the children, Cheri and Gary.

Don and Arlene are considering buying a new home. It's not an expensive home by some standards, but a $70,000 mortgage is nonetheless stretching the monthly principal and interest (P&I) payment of $666.63 for which they qualify. The interest rate at the time of their deliberations is 11 percent.

Although 11 percent is significantly higher than mortgage rates in 1994, we'll use it in our case study for several reasons. The first reason is to prove that interest rate is only one factor in determining whether the three equity criteria fall into the blue, pink, or red zones. Furthermore, since the blue, pink, and red zones are presented in Table 1 for every interest rate between 6 percent and 13 percent, the specimen mortgage of 11 percent doesn't sway the results one way or another. (This will become clearer as we proceed.) Second, rates closer to 10 percent are historically a better long-term benchmark. Finally, other factors are equally important as the interest rate in determining the starting point of the blue, pink, and red zones and whether a particular mortgage is smart, hardworking debt. Everything considered, the Cliftons' 11 percent mortgage will serve quite nicely as a case study.

Purchasing Power

Purchasing power, our first criterion, is different from borrowing power. Borrowing power is the ability of the monthly payment to command or support a certain loan amount through interest expense. Purchasing power, on the other hand, is the monthly payment's contribution to equity ownership. This is measured by the amount of principal contained in each payment. The goal is to secure optimum purchasing power yet stay within the limitation of available resources.

Table 1 reports the average purchasing power of the monthly payment, expressed as a percentage. Its essential purpose is to reveal how hard your money is working. The equity perspective isn't antidebt; it's pro-hardworking-debt. Debt that's working hard to build equity ownership is also smart debt. Remember that the objective is to select a mortgage that is smart, hardworking debt.

Each zone is five years long. (Lenders typically make mortgage loans in five-year increments.) Six zones are reported in this table, totaling a 30-year mortgage. This table and all others like it are read from left to right. Zone 1 reports the first five years of payments on a 30-year mortgage. Zone 6 is the last five years of payment. A home buyer who is considering a 15-year mortgage will have to look at the purchasing power reported in zone 4, because it is 15 years from the finish line. A 20-year mortgage starts in zone 3, and so forth.

The blue zone starts when 50 percent of the monthly payment purchases equity ownership. There are many reasons for the 50 percent point. It's at this point that the monthly payment is both supporting the outstanding loan balance and purchasing equity ownership (i.e., it's the balance point between the debt and equity perspectives). Another reason is the relatively short time after hitting this point that the mortgage is completely paid off—the ultimate equity-building goal. In the case of Don and Arlene's 11 percent mortgage, the 50 percent point is reached less than 10 years before the mortgage is completely repaid. The objective is to reach the 50 percent point as soon as possible.

The actual tables aren't color-coded because to do so would be more confusing than helpful. The blue, pink, and red zones shift around in such a way that it would be visually distracting. Besides, since you're probably only interested in one or two interest rates it's easy enough to see where the zones begin and end.

Table 1

Purchasing Power

Interest Rate	Zones					
	1	2	3	4	5	6
13.0	.03	.06	.11	.20	.38	.73
12.0	.04	.07	.12	.23	.41	.75
11.0	.05	.09	.15	.26	.44	.77
10.0	.07	.11	.18	.29	.48	.78
9.0	.09	.13	.21	.33	.51	.80
8.0	.11	.17	.25	.37	.55	.82
7.0	.15	.21	.30	.42	.59	.84
6.0	.19	.26	.35	.47	.64	.86

As promised earlier, Table 1 also clarifies why an 11 percent interest rate is perfectly acceptable for illustrative purposes. Notice how a 6 percent mortgage shifts to the blue zone only one five-year period earlier than a much higher 11 percent mortgage. Thus a lower interest rate does have an effect, but not as profound as commonly believed.

This observation will be reinforced as we review the other two criteria of the equity perspective.

The pink zone represents average purchasing power of 30 to 50 percent. In this zone your payments are contributing some principal to equity ownership yet not a powerful amount. In the case of a 9 percent mortgage it takes the first 15 years of a 30-year mortgage even to reach the pink zone. Usually only one five-year period elapses between the pink and blue zones.

The red zones represent contributions of less than 30 percent to principal. The monthly payment is obviously doing little more than supporting the outstanding loan balance and hoping that appreciation will bail it out for paying a lot of interest each month. There are other justifications, such as income tax deductions, yet there can be no doubt that the red zones contribute little to equity ownership.

In summary:

> Blue zones—50 percent purchasing power or more.
> Pink zones—30 to 50 percent of purchasing power.
> Red zones—Less than 30 percent purchasing power.

In the case of Don and Arlene's 11 percent mortgage, purchasing power hits the blue zone in zone 5, when approximately half of their $666* monthly P&I payment, or $333 per month, goes toward principal. Figure 1 graphs the purchasing power of Don and Arlene's mortgage payment. As mentioned earlier, to penetrate the maze of information that makes up a 30-year mortgage repayment schedule, all graphs and tables have been broken down into bite-sized portions of six five-year periods. The data for each period have been averaged into a single percentage or dollar amount. Thus you have only six pieces of data to consider for an entire 30-year mortgage.

---

*For ease of calculation, the $666.63 monthly payment will be rounded *down* to $666. Elsewhere figures are rounded as is customary.

Figure 1

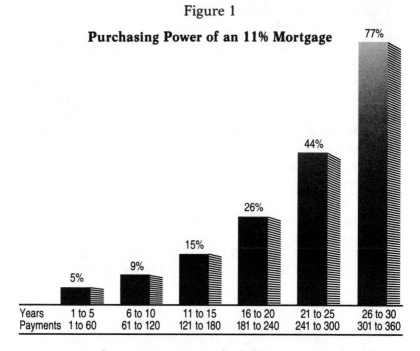

Purchasing Power of an 11% Mortgage

| Years | 1 to 5 | 6 to 10 | 11 to 15 | 16 to 20 | 21 to 25 | 26 to 30 |
| Payments | 1 to 60 | 61 to 120 | 121 to 180 | 181 to 240 | 241 to 300 | 301 to 360 |

Notice that a repayment schedule is an ever-changing arithmetic equation when viewed from an equity perspective. It's not flat or fixed as implied by the constant interest rate and monthly payment. Moreover, these changes are so dramatic that an amortized mortgage can be said to have a split personality. One personality is fat, lazy debt. The other is smart, hardworking debt. These shifting relationships show that it is the laws of arithmetic that stack the majority of interest in the front of the schedule. These laws will be explained in the next chapter.

This graph holds true for all 11 percent mortgages regardless of the loan amount. As you can see, Don and Arlene's monthly mortgage payment hits near the 50 percent point and starts earning real purchasing power in zone 5. Their $666 monthly payment receives an average credit of $293 (.44 × $666) for principal. In zone 6, which is only 5 years from the end of their 30-year mortgage, the average has shot up to $513 (.77 × $666) for principal. These last two zones are the blue zones, where their monthly mortgage payments have clout and are buying real home ownership. In contrast to the blue zones, the first 20 years of mortgage payments are lazy with interest expense. These are the red zones. There is a very small pink zone in an 11 percent mortgage. Rather than buying a home, these 20 years of payments are merely renting money and losing time in the process. Unfortunately, we no longer have the luxury of wasting 20 years of a career on such an expense.

The debt perspective fails to see the shifting nature of an amortization schedule as it relates to purchasing power or any other equity criterion. Not surprisingly, we're advised to take advantage of refinancing opportunities and push the monthly payment to its lowest possible level. Even though this tactic pushes us back to the beginning of zone 1, where our purchasing power is nil, it's still conventional wisdom. We may look like geniuses if appreciation runs in our favor and we cash out in time, but this is a dangerous tactic. The danger, of course, is that just the opposite will happen. All the money has been spent on mortgage payments, appreciation falters, and we're left holding an empty bag. Rather than refinancing for a lower monthly payment, the alternative is to take advantage of the lower interest rate to take a shorter-term mortgage, which may save a decade or more in reaching the blue zone. (For example, if a 7 percent mortgage became available to the Cliftons, they could reduce their monthly payment by $200 by taking out a new 30-year mortgage. *But* they would be back in the lazy-debt red zone. If they decided to continue making roughly the same monthly payment, they could take out a 15-year mortgage, which would put them immediately closer to the equity-building blue zone!) This alternative also increases the purchasing power of our monthly payment and transforms our mortgage into smart debt.

Before proceeding further, it might be helpful to spend a little time exploring the vocabulary, arithmetic, and logic of these graphs. We've already discussed some of the material, but a refresher is always useful with new information.

A *zone* refers to one of the six 5-year periods that comprise a 30-year mortgage. Zone 1 is the first 5 years of payments, and each successive 5-year period is numbered accordingly. Even though these graphs are read from left to right, starting with payment 1, they're actually created the opposite way, from right to left. A 5-year mortgage would have only a single zone, which would be zone 6 with purchasing power of 77 percent. Purchasing power, as you recall, is the amount of a payment that goes toward paying the principal of the loan. A 15-year mortgage would have three zones, numbers 4, 5, and 6, with purchasing power of 26 percent, 44 percent, and 77 percent, respectively. Accordingly, the initial zone of a 15-year mortgage has purchasing power of 26 percent, not the 5 percent of a 30-year mortgage.

The numerical figure, such as 44 percent, represents an *average* percentage or dollar amount. Being an average, half of the purchasing power in zone 5 is higher than the average of 44 percent, and the other half is lower. The fact that half of the purchasing power is higher than 44 percent is the reason zone 5 is considered hardworking debt. The 50 percent point is actually about seven years from the end of the mortgage.

There are several steps in determining the purchasing power of each zone. Step 1 is to total the monthly principal and interest payments for the 60-month period. For example, the Clifton's $666.63 multiplied by 60 months totals almost $40,000 of constant payments. Step 2 is to learn the amount of principal scheduled to be repaid during that same 5-year period, the process for which is described in the next paragraph. In this example, $1,985 of principal is scheduled to be repaid in zone 1. In step 3 we divide the total constant payments into the amount of principal repayment. For example, divide $40,000 into $1,985, and the answer is 5 percent of purchasing power.

Although it's not yet time for an official coffee break, I highly recommend doing this exercise now on your own mortgage. There's nothing like your own money to make a topic come alive. Additionally, this information will have a direct use later, when we tie retirement financing together with home financing.

There are two easy ways to discover the amount of principal repayment for each five-year period of your mortgage. One is by using an amortization schedule. Simply locate the outstanding balance at the end of payments 60, 120, and so on and subtract that balance from the previous amount. For example, the scheduled balance after five years of payments on Don and Arlene's $70,000 mortgage is $68,015. This means $1,985 has been credited to principal. The balance of the $40,000 the Cliftons have paid over these five years went to interest expense. To determine purchasing power, now divide $40,000 into $1,985, for an answer of 5 percent. Next time, at payment 120, subtract that balance from the previous $68,015; that is the new amount of principal repayment.

The other way to learn the amount of principal repayment is to look in a book of mortgage tables. In the book you'll find a *Loan Progress Chart* for each interest rate. After year 5 on a 30-year mortgage, for example, the remaining balance is .971 percent. Multiply the original balance by this factor, and the product is $2,030. Because each method rounds the numbers involved, the results will be slightly different; however, both methods work equally well.

You needn't worry that arithmetic will be a stumbling block in making an informed decision when selecting the ideal mortgage for your personal situation. In the event you detest arithmetic, there's an order form in the back of this book for software, sensibly priced, that will do all these calculations for you. I will also do a number of other things, which we haven't discussed yet.

Truthfully, though, arithmetic is always easier done than explained. For that reason, and because you have a vested interest in the information, I highly recommend that you take a moment and experiment with learning the purchasing power of your mortgage. You might be surprised to discover you already know more than you think you do.

Interest Expense: True Cost

There are two definitions for the cost of a mortgage: the cost of *supporting debt* and the cost of *buying equity.* They are dramatically different from one another. The cost of supporting debt is represented by the interest "rate." The cost of buying ownership is represented by interest "expense." The interest rate is an arithmetic percentage, while *interest expense* refers to the amount of *cash* paid in interest or, more specifically, the total amount of interest paid per $1 of principal. Since buying equity is the objective, interest expense is considered the true cost of your mortgage.

As mentioned at the end of Chapter 2, I first became aware of the distinction between an interest rate and interest expense when I read the 1886 book *Safe Methods of Business,* which contends that the true cost of a loan can be measured only by the actual amount of *cash* paid in interest expense. So if $50 of interest expense is required to repay a $100 loan, its true cost is 50 percent, regardless of the stated interest rate. This definition of true cost ignores time, such as in an annual rate. It presumes that cost is more important than time. Corporations and lenders have unlimited time. Real people have only a limited amount of time and cash. Indeed, cash instead of interest expense and principal/equity instead of the loan balance are the proper measuring sticks when buying ownership is the primary objective of your mortgage.

The difference between interest rate and interest expense is dramatic. An 8 percent mortgage, which is presumed to cost $.08 on $1 of principal, may in fact have an interest expense of 800 percent, because it may really cost an average high of $8 of interest expense for every $1 of principal!

Using true cost is a complete reversal from the way most people are accustomed to measuring the cost of their mortgage. Most people are fooled by a "cheap" 8 percent annual interest rate. But knowing that the actual cost may be closer to 800 percent enables us to decide whether a prospective mortgage *is* actually affordable. This perspective also allows us to measure the dramatic shifts in interest expense between the beginning and end of the repayment schedule. This, in turn, allows us to locate the blue, pink, and red zones of a prospective mortgage's true cost.

The blue zone, in fact, starts when the true cost of buying equity is an average of $1 of interest expense per $1 of principal (when 50 percent of your $2 payment is going toward principal). This is the point where there is a good balance between the debt and equity perspectives, where the cost begins to drop dramatically, and where the time value of money honestly begins to work to your advantage. Naturally, your objective is to reach the blue zone as quickly as possible.

You can discover the true cost of your mortgage alternatives by referring to Table 2 on the following page.

Inspecting a mortgage from an equity perspective is a fascinating experience. Not only does it eliminate all mystery; it also sheds new light on the dynamics of the repayment schedule. Notice, for instance, that the cost of a 6 percent mortgage during just the first five years is $4.18 for every dollar repaid. The cost of a 12 percent mortgage, which appears to be twice as large, actually has a true cost of $25.42. This means that it's really six times more expensive than a 6 percent mortgage. Yet by the time both mortgages reach the last zone the difference has been reduced to 33 cents versus 16 cents. Even though there's still a 100 percent difference between them, the difference is immaterial in terms of dollars and cents. These shadings and interpretations of true cost are additional reasons why only you

Table 2

True Cost

Interest Rate	Zones					
	1	2	3	4	5	6
13.00	$33.59	$17.12	$8.49	$3.97	$1.61	$0.37
12.50	29.50	15.21	7.70	3.67	1.51	0.35
12.00	25.42	13.54	7.01	3.41	1.43	0.33
11.50	22.06	12.01	6.34	3.14	1.34	0.32
11.00	19.15	10.66	5.74	2.90	1.26	0.30
10.50	16.62	9.45	5.19	2.67	1.18	0.29
10.00	14.36	8.34	4.67	2.45	1.10	0.27
9.50	12.41	7.35	4.21	2.24	1.02	0.26
9.00	10.72	6.49	3.78	2.05	0.95	0.25
8.50	9.23	5.70	3.39	1.87	0.88	0.23
8.00	7.93	4.99	3.02	1.70	0.81	0.22
7.50	6.79	4.36	2.69	1.54	0.75	0.20
7.00	5.80	3.80	2.38	1.39	0.68	0.19
6.50	4.94	3.29	2.10	1.24	0.62	0.17
6.00	4.18	2.84	1.85	1.11	0.56	0.16

can determine the value of these trade-offs. Now, perhaps for the first time, you have the information and insight to make informed decisions.

The pink zone is where interest expense is between $1 and $2. This still isn't a cheap mortgage, yet it's in the affordable range. In the case of a 7.5 percent mortgage, the pink zone starts somewhere between zones 3 and 4. If we get a 7.5 percent mortgage and select a 15-year mortgage, we start immediately in the pink zone. If we select a 30-year term instead, we have to make 15 years of payments before hitting the pink zone. Fifteen years is a very long time.

The red zones are everything higher than $2 of interest expense. And even though the zone 1 interest expense of a 6 percent mortgage is six times less than a 13 percent mortgage, you shouldn't be fooled by the noticeably lower true cost. Interest expense of $6.79 for a 7.5 percent mortgage is still an effective true cost of 679 percent. Makes the 18 percent cost of many credit cards seem pretty cheap, doesn't it? (As a factual matter, the interest expense of credit cards, or automobile loans for that matter, should be calculated over a five-year period to determine their true cost; then compare it to the cost of a mortgage. Even so, the mortgage is still much more expensive.)

In summary:

Blue zones—$1 of interest expense, or less.

Pink zones—$1 to $2 of interest expense.

Red zones—$2 or more of interest expense.

When you look at the red zone, it's obvious that a person has to be extraordinarily lucky to pay $19 of interest expense, as the Cliftons would at the beginning of their 11 percent 30-year mortgage, and still come out ahead of the financial game. Figure 2 on the following page details the true cost of Don and Arlene's mortgage. (This graph holds true for all 11 percent mortgages.) When Don and Arlene look at this true cost graph, they'll discover the blue zone starts somewhere between zone 5 and zone 6. The pink zone starts somewhere between zones 4 and 5.

Notice how true cost is cut almost in half in each successive zone. The slope is so steep it looks like a ski jump. The configuration of this graph is just the opposite, or inverse, relationship of the purchasing power graph. Purchasing power starts extremely low and finishes quite high. True cost, on the other hand, starts exceedingly high and finishes quite low. This is no coincidence. Since the monthly mortgage payment is constant, it goes to satisfy interest first, and the remaining amount goes to principal. The higher the interest, the less principal, and vice versa. To succeed in buying equity ownership, you must be situated where interest expense is low and purchasing power is high.

There's another observation to be made about the dramatic shift in the true cost of buying equity—*it is the length of the repayment schedule that adds the greater cost to a mortgage, not the interest rate.* If Don and Arlene had

Figure 2
True Cost of an 11% Mortgage

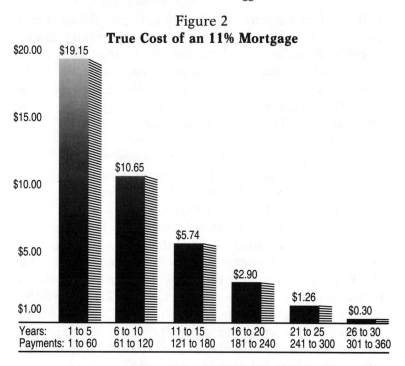

| Years: | 1 to 5 | 6 to 10 | 11 to 15 | 16 to 20 | 21 to 25 | 26 to 30 |
| Payments: | 1 to 60 | 61 to 120 | 121 to 180 | 181 to 240 | 241 to 300 | 301 to 360 |

started with a 15-year mortgage, for instance, they would have started at $2.90 of interest expense and proceeded down to $.30. Instead, they started at $19 of interest expense on the very same 11 percent mortgage. Starting at $19 instead of $2.90 on the same 11 percent mortgage proves it's actually the length of the repayment term that adds the most cost for buying equity ownership. Perhaps they could trade a larger down payment for a shorter-term mortgage. This would leave their monthly payment at $666. Or perhaps they could wait for rates to drop down to 9 percent, or maybe they could pay a one-point fee and buy a lower rate which would allow them to afford a shorter-term mortgage. (The objective is to shorten the term of the mortgage, not to "save'" a percentage point or two.)

Rather than managing interest *rates*, selecting a mortgage from the equity perspective requires that we manage interest *expense*. Instead of adopting the lender's definition of true cost, we must adopt the consumer's definition. In place of borrowing time, we must manage cash. In sum, instead of managing debt, we must learn to build equity.

Initial Gain/Opportunity Loss

Initial gain/opportunity loss may be the biggest trade-off of all. It's certainly the most well hidden. Hidden within it are both the debt and equity perspectives. The *initial gain* is the increase in borrowing power that you get by taking out a longer-term loan. This reflects the debt perspective. The *opportunity loss*, which reflects the equity perspective, is the cost of capital and the loss of earnings for that increase—the cash that you ultimately lose to gain initial borrowing power. (The reason a loss is part of the equity perspective is that every dollar of loss is one dollar less going into a nest egg.) In other words, taking out a longer-term mortgage might enable you to buy a more expensive home *now* but at a great cost *later*—possibly so great that it would have prohibited you from selecting that mortgage if you had known about this cost up front. Knowing the initial gain/opportunity loss trade-off of a prospective mortgage gives you more of the insight needed to decide whether the extra borrowing power is worth it. Similar to purchasing power and true cost, this criterion is graded from blue to red zones, with pink in between.

Initial Gain. There are two aspects to the phrase *initial gain. Initial* implies that the additional borrowing power gained by extending the mortgage term is an immediate reward. It may help you qualify for the loan and thus accomplish its greatest mission on the day you close the loan. It may give you time to catch your financial breath by lowering the monthly payment to the absolute minimum when the expenses of a new home are the highest. It may also help you attempt to leverage for appreciation. Even though none of these rewards are of long-term benefit, they are often the short-term necessities of life.

Gain refers to the increase in the borrowing power that you get for each five-year period added to the repayment term of your mortgage. For instance, you can borrow more money by extending the repayment term from 25 years to 30 years. This gain in borrowing power is in fact the benefit of taking a longer-term mortgage. Calculating the initial gain on Don and Arlene's proposed mortgage is a simple matter. Table 3 reports the initial gains on Don and Arlene's borrowing power of $666.63 P&I per month, at 11 percent annual interest.

First, go back to the purchasing power graph in Figure 1. Now think in terms of how the repayment schedule of a mortgage is originally constructed—it's built from right to left. For example, a 5-year mortgage is represented by the last 5 years of mortgage payments (zone 6), which for the Cliftons means principal of more than $30,000. A 10-year mortgage contains zones 5 and 6, with their combined borrowing power at $48,390: $30,654 for the 5-year loan plus $17,736 for extending the mortgage term to 10 years. And so forth: to find out how much they could borrow altogether for a given loan term, the Cliftons simply add up the gains from the 5-year term to the term in question. (If you add the amounts in all 6 columns, you'll get their $70,000 total mortgage amount.)

Table 3

Initial Gain: The Cliftons

Term					
30-Year	25-Year	20-Year	15-Year	10-Year	5-Year
$1,985	$3,432	$5,934	$10,259	$17,736	$30,654

You may notice that the initial gain of each additional 5-year period is cut almost in half from the previous period. Taking out a 20-year loan rather than one with a 15-

year term gives the Cliftons only $5,934 additional initial gain, when the previous gain was $10,259. In total, the initial gain between a 15-year and a 30-year mortgage is only $11,351 ($5,934 + $3,432 + $1,985). In other words, Don and Arlene can borrow $58,649 on a 15-year mortgage and $70,000 if they take a 30-year mortgage. Since they need a $70,000 mortgage, they may indeed have little choice but a 30-year mortgage. Sound familiar?

The initial gain in the last zone is a mere $1,985. This means that five years of mortgage payments were added to the repayment schedule in exchange for a gain in borrowing power of $1,985. The corollary is that it will also require five years of monthly payments to repay this $1,985 initial gain. The fact that the initial gain is only $1,985 is neither good nor bad, however, until it is compared against the opportunity loss for that gain. Perhaps they'll offer $1,985 less for the house and qualify for a 25-year mortgage, thus saving $40,000 in mortgage payments.

Prior to calculating the opportunity loss, this is a good time to take a break and measure the initial gain on your prospective mortgages. If you haven't yet constructed your own graph on purchasing power, I recommend doing so now. The initial gain in borrowing power between a 15-year and a 30-year mortgage is an especially vital piece of information. It will be used a number of times in the future. Don't be surprised if initial gain is less than you imagine.

The baseline for measuring the value of the initial gain against the total opportunity loss for that gain is a 15-year mortgage. A 15-year term is considered the most practical baseline because it's the most frequent repayment term, next to 30-year mortgages, when home buyers are comparing different mortgages.

Opportunity Loss

Whether an initial gain is worth the opportunity loss can be evaluated only after you compare the full cost of the initial gain, which includes the loss of capital and also future earnings on it. In some cases the immediate gain may be absolutely necessary and thus justify an opportunity loss that will be dramatic in the future. In other cases the cost may be considered too great and not worth the gain. Ultimately, only you can be the judge. Still, some guidelines may prove helpful.

A blue zone represents an opportunity loss no more than five times greater than the initial gain. This may seem generous. After all, it's a cost of 500 percent! Yet I assure you it's not all that extravagant. Considering that it's over a number of years, there's probably enough time to recapture the cost with normal earnings. Can the opportunity loss be paid by normal earnings, or will it require extraordinary means? That is the fundamental question. The answer to this question requires looking down the road and making a realistic guess of your future earnings. Don't be too optimistic; be conservative in your estimate. This challenge is further compounded by the cumulative growth in the opportunity loss. A 10-year opportunity loss, for instance, is more than twice the size of a 5-year loss. That's because compound interest expense has had more time to do its damage.

The pink zone represents an opportunity loss between 5 and 7½ times the size of the initial gain. Though only a 50 percent increase, the pink zone is increasingly difficult to compensate exclusively through normal earnings. A greater reliance must now be placed on appreciation to make up the loss of capital and forgone earnings.

The red zones are opportunity losses greater than 7½ times the initial gain. It's virtually certain that the red zones will depend on appreciation to bail them out of this loss. Trade-offs 7½ times larger than the initial gain are a sign that a mortgage was selected according to the debt perspective. Perhaps there was no other choice at the time. Don't lose hope if this is your situation. Selecting an equity-wise mortgage from the outset is the optimum but is not always possible. Sometimes people are forced to accept a trade-off in the red zones. If this is your situation, there's an opportunity in the future to reverse the effects of this selection and transform a lazy mortgage into hardworking debt.

In summary:

Blue zone—Five times opportunity loss, or less.

Pink zone—Five to seven and a half times opportunity loss.

Red zone—Seven and a half times opportunity loss, or more.

You can determine the opportunity loss of your mortgage alternatives by referring to Table 4. The factors represented in this table are cumulative. In other words, the opportunity loss for a 25-year mortgage accounts for a 10-year extension over the baseline 15-year mortgage, not just the 5-year increase from the previous 20-year term. After all, you can't have a 25-year mortgage without having a 20-year term as part of it. The factors (rounded to the nearest quarter point) apply to all mortgages in their respective interest rate, regardless of loan amount. Since this is a fairly linear arithmetic equation, you may interpolate between the whole percentage rates to discover the proper factors for other interest rates.

Table 4

Opportunity Loss

Interest Rate	30-Year Term 15-Year Loss	25-Year Term 10-Year Loss	20-Year Term 5-Year Loss
13%	30.75	15.50	11.75
12	25.00	14.75	9.75
11	20.25	13.00	8.25
10	16.50	10.75	7.00
9	13.50	9.00	6.00
8	11.00	7.25	5.00
7	8.75	6.00	4.25
6	7.25	5.25	3.50

Similar to purchasing power and interest expense, the opportunity loss table is quite dynamic. The effect of interest rates, though, is much greater on opportunity loss than on purchasing power. That's because the time value of money has entered the equation. This time value of money is another consideration that proves once again that selecting a mortgage is not a matter of finding one answer but of evaluating a series of trade-offs. Each home buyer must judge what's most important for his or her situation.

The Opportunity Loss for Don and Arlene Clifton. In exchange for the initial gain of $11,351 Don and Arlene agreed to make 15 years of extra mortgage payments. As you can see from Table 4, the factor associated with a 30-year mortgage, which is a 15-year loss, is 20.25. This means the opportunity loss is 20.25 times greater than the initial gain. The approximate product of $11,351 and 20.25 is an astonishing $230,000!

This opportunity loss is comprised of two parts. The capital loss portion of it is attributed to the loss of $666.63 per month for 180 months (15 years). These extra payments total almost $120,000. The other half is the lost opportunity to earn 15 years of income or interest on that capital. The earning value of capital is more than a possibility or an opportunity; it's a certainty. Financial markets take the word *time* and translate it to mean "interest." Either you're earning it or you're paying it. Presuming these 180 mortgage payments would have been put into a safe investment vehicle earning 8 percent per annum (the conventional long-term earnings rate), the lost earnings amount to an additional $110,000. Add the loss of these earnings to the loss of capital, and the total loss is a staggering $230,000.

Don and Arlene are astounded. They never realized an initial gain of $11,351 was scheduled to cost $230,000. And no one told them either. Mortgage lenders never look at it this way. They look only at the annual interest rate and monthly payment. Realtors and other real estate profession-

als are so steeped in the debt tradition that they don't notice
it either. Even if they did, their job is not to counsel buyers.
Home buyers don't pay their salaries; home sellers do. In
many instances it's even illegal for real estate agents to
offer advice that may be contrary to their sellers' best
interests. Even financial planners are more concerned with
managing debt, taxes, and investment securities than with
their clients' home investment. Only the independent mortgage adviser, which is a new and emerging profession,
doesn't have a conflict of interest and can provide this kind
of advice.

An opportunity loss this large explains why it's nearly
impossible to compensate for the full cost of the initial gain
out of normal earnings. Appreciation—and a lot of it—is
necessary to break even on such a high opportunity loss. It
also explains why after 10 years of mortgage payments a
homeowner can go broke if the real estate market goes
down 10 percent or more. Moreover, it explains why it's so
difficult to save money. Such an expensive opportunity loss
consumes so much money that it's all but impossible to
build a nest egg for retirement, college tuition, or just your
peace of mind.

Fortunately, not all opportunity losses are this expensive. Nor must the Cliftons agree to this trade-off. They
have other alternatives. They can select a shorter-term
mortgage, such as a 20-year term, where the opportunity
loss factor is reduced to 8.25 times the initial gain (see
Table 4). Since the initial gain for this 5-year period is
$5,934 (see Table 3), their opportunity loss would be
$48,956. Still not cheap, but a far cry from $230,000.
Another choice would be to wait for interest rates to drop
and select an 8 percent 30-year mortgage, which has an
opportunity loss factor of 11. Viewed from this perspective,
an 8 percent mortgage has an initial gain/opportunity loss
trade-off almost half that of the 11 percent mortgage. Also
notice that the factor for a 25-year term is reduced to 7.25.
Worth thinking about, isn't it?

The ability to measure the dollar amount of these trade-offs is a major benefit of the initial gain/opportunity loss criterion. For instance, imagine the new considerations about financing $1,000 of kitchen appliances when you now realize they'll cost $20,000 by the time they're paid off. And what about financing the closing costs? No matter Don and Arlene's ultimate decision; they can now do so on an informed basis. Even if they're forced to begin with the most expensive mortgage, they're now armed with good information and won't be shocked to discover the truth many years later, when it may be too late to do something about it. Doing something about it now is an added benefit of the equity perspective.

Coffee Break

Have you ever noticed that topics about money seem to scare most people? Roger Von Oech encountered the same problem and overcame it by thinking about money in the same way a plumber thinks about water. In his book *A Whack on the Side of the Head,* Oech noted that banking jargon seems to be talking about plumbing:

Liquid assets	Solvency	Washed up
Flooding the market	In the pipeline	Floating a loan
Taking a bath	Slush fund	Cash flow
Frozen assets	Capital drain	Currency

I spent several years in a large bank in charge of special projects with the responsibility for solving financial problems. I can testify that bankers definitely use these plumbing terms. So every time you feel overwhelmed by unfamiliar lingo or jargon, just imagine a man sitting behind his desk in coveralls, frantically trying to liquefy some frozen assets that are draining his capital and slowing cash flow to the point where he's taking a bath. Many of them, as you know, got washed up in the flood of loans they floated in the marketplace.

There's nothing like your own money to make a discussion come alive. With that thought in mind, I've prepared a shortcut to help you discover the opportunity loss on a mortgage you might be considering or perhaps already own. This method takes your monthly mortgage payment (principal and interest only) and calculates its value if it is put into a savings account earning 8 percent per annum over 5-year, 10-year, and 15-year periods.

Table 5

Opportunity Loss Shortcut

Deposit Amount	5 Years	10 Years	15 Years
$ 100	$ 7,348	$ 18,294	$ 34,604
200	14,695	36,558	69,207
300	22,043	54,884	103,811
400	29,391	73,178	138,414
500	36,738	91,473	173,018
600	44,086	109,767	207,621
700	51,433	128,056	242,210
800	58,780	146,356	276,811
900	66,129	164,651	311,412
1,000	73,476	182,864	346,035

To determine your opportunity loss, simply approximate your monthly payment in the left column and trace the line across to the amount listed in the 15-year column. Don and Arlene could have interpolated their $666 payment and hit on the $230,000 amount. For payments over $1,000, merely add two amounts together. For example, a $1,300 payment would add $346,035 ($1,000) to $103,811 ($300) for a total of $449,846. An impressive amount of money, especially when you realize it's subtracted from your nest egg.

Now compare the initial gain of your prospective mortgage against the opportunity loss:

Initial Gain   _____

Opportunity Loss   _____

That's right! The opportunity loss of 15 years is probably the exact amount you need to retire. When we calculated that retirement amount in the Coffee Break of the last chapter it probably seemed like a frighteningly large amount of cash. Now you know where your nest egg lay hidden. For most people, 15 years of mortgage payments and the earnings on that capital are a perfect match with the size of nest egg needed to secure their retirement. This isn't a product of arithmetic but the result of human nature. That's because most people buy a house up to their standard of living. It shouldn't come as a surprise, therefore, to realize there's a correlation between the size of their mortgage payment and the size of nest egg needed to preserve that standard of living.

The best news is that you aren't dependent on appreciation after all. If you earn enough income to afford these mortgage payments, you already earn enough income to build a nest egg to retire with the security and peace of mind you deserve.

End of Break

Parallel Track

There is no one perfect mortgage. What is ideal to a young person who is buying a starter home and who is assured of being transferred to another city within the next three years is entirely different from what's considered ideal for a middle-aged couple with two children in grade school who are now buying their third house and plan on spending the rest of their careers in this community. Selecting the mortgage that's ideal for your situation is likewise a series of trade-offs. These trade-offs mean that striking a balance between the debt and equity perspectives is the best approach to making an informed mortgage decision.

There are three common points of comparison between the debt and equity perspectives. The first point concerns the monthly mortgage payment and purchasing power. The debt perspective aims for the lowest possible monthly payment. What is gained by a low monthly payment, however, is lost in purchasing power. The equity perspective strives to obtain the highest purchasing power per month. It believes a homeowner's payment has clout only when 50 percent or more of it is credited to principal reduction. Smart, hardworking debt is considered essential to financial security in the 1990s.

Likewise for the second viewpoint, which concerns the interest rate and interest expense. The debt perspective wants to borrow time as well as money. It thus considers the annual interest rate to be the real cost of borrowing time, as well as the cost of interest on the outstanding balance. The equity perspective doesn't want to borrow time, which it considers the same as losing time; it wants to buy equity ownership. It considers the true cost of buying equity to be the total amount of cash spent on interest expense, irrespective of the amount of time. One dollar of interest expense or less per dollar of equity is the goal. In the viewpoint of debt, time may be on your side and maybe not. The annual inflation and appreciation rate may allow

homeowners to borrow themselves rich and maybe not.
Maybe just the opposite. Viewed from the perspective of
equity, hard-dollar or real equity ownership ensures that
the homeowner will win regardless of outside and uncon-
trollable forces, such as the appreciation rate. The lower the
amount of cash spent on interest expense, the better.

The third point of comparison concerns borrowing
power and the advantages and disadvantages of maximiz-
ing it. The debt perspective intends to leverage the borrowing power of the monthly payment to its maximum level. It
assumes that time is on its side and that whatever may look
expensive today will be cheap tomorrow. Therefore, a long
repayment term is better than a short one, because a homeowner can borrow more money. A 30-year or even 40-year
term is the accepted norm. The equity perspective takes the
opposite viewpoint. It contends that the increased borrowing power is worth it only if it can be recaptured out of
normal earnings. It presumes that time and appreciation
are not on our side and that additional borrowing power
that consumes more than five times its value in extra mortgage payments and lost earnings is an unacceptable trade-
off. *This perspective believes that trading as much as 10 to
20 times the initial gain in borrowing power is where most
people forfeit their nest egg.*

Balancing between the debt and equity perspectives is
the essence of a parallel track strategy. The idea is to consider both points of view in selecting a mortgage. The practical fact of the matter is that most home buyers have limited financial resources, which cannot be forced to grow on
command. Yet these limitations don't diminish the importance of building equity ownership either. Within this context of competing interests the idea is to mix and match
both debt and equity criteria so the eventual decision is
based on the best thinking of both perspectives.

Unbeknown to most people, for instance, is that they
have the ability to swap elements of the debt criteria, such
as points, repayment terms, interest rate, and monthly pay-

ment, for a more desirable effect on purchasing power, interest expense, and opportunity loss. For example, it may be possible to pay a 1 percent fee, known as *points*, in exchange for a lower interest rate, which may permit a borrower to take a 20-year repayment term instead of a 30-year term. (It doesn't take much to achieve this result.) The average starting purchasing power of a 20-year mortgage is three times greater than it is for a 30-year mortgage. Is the swap worth it? Only you can be the judge. From a pure equity viewpoint and given no financial limitations, just the objective of selecting the most equity-wise mortgage, a 10-year repayment term is ideal. Every monthly payment is working hard to build equity. There are still substantial tax deductions. The time value of money is really working to your advantage. Finally, a nest egg built on 20 years of deposits and compound earnings is more than 50 percent bigger than a 15-year nest egg. In the case of Don and Arlene, that means their nest egg would grow to $395,000. As you can readily see, the range and number of possible trade-offs is almost endless. Now aware of the trade-offs for both sides of the coin, you finally have all the information needed to measure and evaluate your prospective mortgages and select the most ideal one for your situation.

The Next Step

If you're like most people, you may not be able to select a mortgage that meets your equity ambitions from the outset. Financial limitations are a part of everyone's life. Don't despair if this is your situation. There is a way to transform an existing red mortgage into a smart blue one. All of the secrets you need to do so are contained in the purchasing power, interest expense, and initial gain/opportunity loss criteria. You didn't know it at the time, but when you learned how to measure these amounts you also learned the keys to reversing the effects of a lazy mortgage.

In a nutshell, you can reverse the negative effects of

your initial choice by giving back the benefits, such as the initial gain in borrowing power, ahead of schedule. In doing so, you recapture the opportunity loss and reposition your monthly payment into the pink and blue zones. For example, if Don and Arlene accelerate repayment of their $11,351 initial gain over a reasonable number of years, they'll recapture their $230,000 opportunity loss. Knowing the amount of initial gain on your individual mortgage tells you the *amount* of principal that is to be accelerated. The proper amount varies according to every mortgage, because the initial gain of every mortgage varies. Purchasing power tells you *when* it must be accelerated. Interest expense tells how *much* principal must be accelerated in a particular month. The name of this strategy is *principal acceleration.*

In addition to transforming an existing mortgage into smart, hardworking debt, principal acceleration preserves many of the benefits of the debt perspective. Foremost is the ability to maximize our borrowing power at the beginning of the mortgage and then transform it into an equity-wise one later. This may be the best of both worlds. Another benefit is that you retain the same appreciation opportunity as someone still leveraged to the hilt in a debt strategy. Appreciation is no higher for a home with high debt than for one with high equity. For instance, if both homes are valued at $100,000 and appreciation of 10 percent occurs, both the leveraged and equity homes appreciate the same $10,000. Furthermore, principal acceleration has little effect on your tax deductions. All the while that you're accelerating principal, you're also making normal mortgage payments, which is still loaded with deductible interest expense. It's not until about zone 5 that it experiences a noticeable drop. You're going to get there sooner or later, so you might as well get there 15 years sooner.

Principal acceleration is also good for America. The equity you build and the cash nest egg you create are building blocks for the prosperity of tomorrow. If only 10 percent of homeowners, for example, pursued such a program, it would put about $40 billion per year into the savings and investment systems. That's only one year! Imagine if they did that year after year for the next 15 years. It might be an old-fashioned notion, but what's good for the average citizen is also good for the country.

Moreover, there are no hidden traps, such as prepayment penalties and other paper dragons. Finally, and in addition to the economic and financial advantages, principal acceleration also provides an emotional one—it safeguards the home sanctuary. Could anything be more important?

A Last Word and Heading On . . .

Selecting an equity-wise mortgage from the outset is a giant step toward adopting an equity strategy. It also fulfills the abundance rule action steps:

Action Step 1. Stop managing debt as your primary financial strategy.
Action Step 2. Avoid unnecessary interest expense.
Action Step 3. Build equity ownership and a cash nest egg.

If it isn't possible to take advantage of this opportunity from the start, your second and ongoing opportunity is to transform a lazy mortgage into a hardworking one via principal acceleration.

Contrary to conventional wisdom, opportunity doesn't knock just once; it actually keeps knocking until we answer the call.

PART II
HOW TO . . .

4
Principal Acceleration

... "But *all* I earn is mine to keep, is it not?" Arkad demanded. "Far from it," Algamish replied. "Do you not pay the garment-maker? Do you not pay the sandal-maker? Do you not pay for the things you eat? Can you live in Babylon without spending? What have you to show for your earnings of the past month? What for the past year? Fool! You pay to everyone but yourself. Dullard, you labor for others. As well be a slave and work for what your master gives you to eat and wear. If you did keep for yourself one-tenth of all you earn, how much would you have in ten years?"

My knowledge of the numbers did not forsake me, and I answered, "As much as I earn in one year."

"You speak but half the truth," he retorted. "Every gold piece you save is a slave to work for you. Every copper it earns is its child that also can earn for you. If you would become wealthy, then what you save must earn, and its children must earn, that all may help to give to you the abundance you crave.

"You think I cheat you for your long night's work," he continued, "but I am paying you a thousand times over if you have the intelligence to grasp the truth I offer you.

"A part of all you earn is yours to keep. It should be not less than a tenth no matter how little you earn. It can be as much more as you can afford. Pay yourself first. Do not buy from the clothes-maker and the sandal-maker more than you can pay out of the rest and still have enough for food and charity and penance to the gods.

"Wealth, like a tree, grows from a tiny seed. The first copper you save is the seed from which your tree of wealth shall grow. The sooner you plant that seed the sooner the tree shall grow. And the more faithfully you nourish and water that tree with consistent savings, the sooner may you bask in contentment beneath its shade."

So saying, he took his tablets and went away. . . .

excerpted from *The Richest Man in Babylon*
by George S. Clason

"Pay yourself first" is a philosophy that has proved itself time and again. So has the idea of saving a 10th of your earnings. Like other magical points, 10 percent seems to be a savings rate that unleashes powerful forces. One may argue it's too high in this modern era of quick credit and ready cash, but that's another matter. Without paying yourself first, which means prior to any other expense, it's extremely difficult to save money. Most people, however, tend to pay themselves *last*. They propose to save whatever is left after their bills are paid. This is a trap! Expenses increase to meet the income available. Predictably, there's never any money left over. If ever money is to be your servant and not your feared master, paying yourself first should be the first order of business. Surprisingly, everyone who has followed this advice since *The Richest Man in Babylon* was first published in 1929 reports living just as well on the remaining 90 percent as when 100 percent was allocated to expenses. There is perhaps no better application of paying yourself first than principal acceleration. It saves 10 times the 10 percent maxim.

Despite the wisdom of keeping a part of all you earn and paying yourself first, it's more a philosophy than an absolute truth. No amount of coaxing or argument will change the mind of someone who believes otherwise. Beliefs about money are strongly held and strongly defended. Marriage counselors, for instance, concur that disagreement over money is the largest single cause of divorce. These beliefs are formed early in childhood. One child squirrels coins away in a secret hiding place and relishes counting them in private. Another child is attracted by the immediacy of candy. Seldom do beliefs change when these children grow up. Those committed to a debt strategy can find a host of events, situations, and possibilities that will bear witness to their belief in the wisdom of debt. Here are just two samples of these counterarguments: If the real estate market is going up, for instance, they say building real equity ownership is unnecessary; besides, it's too slow. On the other hand, if the market is going down, they contend it is foolish to throw good money after bad into a house when its value is diminishing. Likewise for interest rates. If they're high, people say the monthly payment is too high and they can't afford to accelerate principal. If rates are low, the argument is switched around, and they can't afford to get rid of their low monthly payment. And so on and so forth. Other arguments, such as tax deductions, are addressed in Chapter 7. The purpose of mentioning them now is to acknowledge that building real home ownership and creating a cash nest egg are not for everyone, and those people aren't necessarily wrong. For those who desire financial security and peace of mind, though, there is perhaps no better way to apply the equity strategy and pay yourself first than principal acceleration.

Principal acceleration is one of the two major schools within a larger concept known generically as *mortgage prepayment*. The other school within mortgage prepayment is *principal prepayment*. Principal prepayment methods and principal acceleration strategies are as different as blue jays and eagles. Prepayment methods, which are based on the debt perspective, define the desired amount of monthly prepayment and let results fall where they may. In contrast, a principal acceleration strategy defines the desired results and lets the monthly prepayment fall where it needs to. Between the two choices, your chances of building genuine home ownership and a nest egg of your own is far superior with principal acceleration.

Mortgage Prepayment

Mortgage prepayment was popularized when the Depression generation began buying houses again in the 1940s. Prior to the Depression of the 1930s, there were usually only 5-year and 10-year mortgages. Afterward, the 30-year mortgage was standard. The idea of being in debt for 30 years, however, was inconceivable to these people. My own parents and all our neighbors practiced some form of mortgage prepayment. No one knew precisely how it worked, or what the results would be, but they knew it was somehow shortening the term of their mortgage. By now everyone knows a little something about mortgage prepayment. They usually know the mortgage will be paid off sometime early in the unforeseen and distant future. Understandably, they also think that mortgage payments are eliminated from the back of the schedule and that they save $.10 of interest expense, for instance, on a 10 percent mortgage, both of which are incorrect. What they don't realize is that mortgage prepayment is usually based on the debt perspective.

Principal acceleration is based on the equity perspective. It has everything that prepayment lacks: strategy, objectives, goals, budgets, timetables, tracking systems, and so forth—all of which are tied back to the initial gain in each homeowner's mortgage. Prior to exploring principal acceleration, though, it will be useful to review conventional prepayment methods and the financial reason why mortgage prepayment works in the first place.

Principal Prepayment Methods

Conventional prepayment methods are driven foremost by whatever money is conveniently left over after other expenses and a general desire to pay off the mortgage early and save interest. These are not specific goals, because they're based on and calculated from the debt perspective. Since people still believe the annual interest rate is the true cost, they think they're saving $.11 per dollar of prepayment on an 11 percent mortgage, for instance. The *amount* of prepayment doesn't matter under this perspective, because $1 of prepayment saves the same $.11. Nor does it matter *when* the prepayment is made because it too saves a constant amount of interest throughout the life of the mortgage. There's no distinction between the lazy debt or the equity zones of the mortgage. They don't recognize the 60-times power curve in the true cost of the mortgage. Nor do they realize a dollar prepaid against zone 1 eliminates an average of $19 of interest expense, while a dollar prepaid against zone 6 eliminates only $.30 of interest expense (see Table 2). When one fails to recognize and incorporate these insights into an overall strategy, all methods appear to yield the same results. Hence the only issue is convenience.

Even if these conventional methods fail to strike when the opportunity is greatest, they are still far better than doing nothing at all. Each of them yields beneficial results.

Constant Payment Method

The constant payment method calls for prepaying the same amount of principal every month, usually in even increments such as $50, $75, $100, and so forth. The foremost advantage of this method is utter simplicity. The same amount is added to the normal mortgage payment, and arithmetic is permitted to take care of the rest. The results of the constant method can also be predicted. The most intelligent approach to constant prepayments is repaying the 30-year mortgage according to principal and interest payments for a 15-year schedule. There are any number of inexpensive computer software programs that will recalculate your repayment schedule based on a constant amount of prepayment.

The disadvantage of this method is that it saves less and less money as you proceed down the repayment schedule. It treats both halves of the mortgage as though they were equal. The other disadvantage is that most people don't have a computer system and can't run a new repayment schedule, so they're flying blind and trusting that everything will work out OK.

Variable Payment Method

The variable payment method calls for adding whatever is left over after the rest of the monthly bills are paid. It has the advantage of being easy, as does the constant payment method, but it also has the same disadvantage of failing to save as much interest expense as possible, plus the added disadvantage of being unpredictable. Since the amount changes every month, it's impossible to know where you're headed, how much you will save, how much earlier you'll pay off the mortgage, whether the prepayments are being applied properly, and so forth. Yet it's better than doing nothing at all.

Next-Month Principal Method

This method calls for prepaying the principal scheduled for the subsequent payment along with the current payment. The goal is to eliminate half of the payments by eliminating every other scheduled payment. Thus a 30-year mortgage is supposed to be paid off 15 years early. An advantage is predictability. Since you're prepaying every other scheduled payment, you can simply look at the repayment schedule and plan ahead.

This method, however, forgets to consider the increasing cost of prepayment. Using the purchasing power percentages in Table 1 and the monthly payment of $666, the average cost to eliminate one mortgage payment at the beginning of the Cliftons' repayment schedule is a mere $33. As soon as 50 percent of the original balance has been repaid, however, the average cost increases to $510. Obviously, prepayments that cost $33 are better than prepayments that cost $510. Yet this consideration is ignored. Not surprisingly, it's typically abandoned long before anyone eliminates a full 15 years of payments.

Lump Sum Method

Using the lump sum method, the borrower plans on making periodic large payments. One example of a lump sum method is making one prepayment per year equal to the size of your normal monthly payment. By virtue of making 13 payments instead of the normal 12, it's conceivable to pay off the loan 10 years early. The lump sum method is the method of choice for people such as farmers, owners of vacation businesses, and so forth who receive their incomes seasonally.

The disadvantage is that it takes a tremendous amount of self-discipline to make a payment that large once a year. Who's got extra money during the holiday period, for example? Finally, this method also assumes that you'll prepay throughout the life of the mortgage. Few people have the stamina and discipline to implement this kind of program over 20 years.

Biweekly Method

A variation of the constant payment method is the conversion of your fixed mortgage into a biweekly mortgage. A biweekly mortgage is one where one-half of the monthly payment is paid every two weeks. The advantage of this plan is that it appears that you're paying no more than usual, and yet you save 8 to 10 years' worth of mortgage payments. Biweekly mortgages work because there are actually 26 biweeks in the year as opposed to 24 semi-months; thus a lump sum payment equal to a 13th monthly payment is actually made.

Normally, biweekly mortgages must be set up from the beginning. However, a growing number of companies are getting into the business of converting your existing monthly mortgage to a biweekly plan through the use of an escrow account. They charge an up-front fee of 1 percent of the anticipated savings over the life of the mortgage. This conversion plan calls for paying half of your mortgage payment into the escrow account every two weeks, out of which it pays your mortgage once a month. At the end of the year the escrow account will have a surplus to make the lump sum payment. There are at least two disadvantages to converting your monthly mortgage into a biweekly plan. One is that it normally takes about five years to recover the 1 percent fee charged. Since most people move about every five years, there's barely enough time to recover the fee before it's time to move again. Furthermore, and more important, a biweekly plan is implemented over the entire life of the loan and is effectively spinning its wheels in the back of the mortgage.

Each of these conventional prepayment methods has its advantages and disadvantages. They all save time and money. But they also leave half of the savings on the table. At the root of their disadvantages is the belief that the cost of a mortgage is represented by the annual interest rate and therefore it doesn't matter *when* the mortgage is prepaid or by what *amount*. Nor do they have a strategy designed to produce specific results. Their focus is almost entirely on the convenience of the monthly payment. Principal prepayment methods fail to be impressive and are usually abandoned long before they're completed.

Despite their shortcomings, these prepayment methods are a marvelous way of unlocking the chains of a 30-year mortgage.

Why Prepayment Works

From time to time it's been noted that you don't need to worry why prepayment is allowed, how the numbers work, the reason arithmetic takes care of the rest, why you are in complete charge, or how your gain is not the lender's loss. You've taken these proclamations on faith. Now, though, it's time to show you the financial justification for these assertions.

Most people think they're required to repay their mortgage according to the original repayment schedule. Actually, the repayment schedule reflects only the *minimum* repayment requirements. After sifting through all the boilerplate in the note and deed of trust and the promissory note on your mortgage, there are only four essential requirements in your documents:

1. You must pay back the *entire* loan amount.
2. You can take no *longer* than the specified term.
3. You can pay no *less* than the specified monthly payment.
4. Interest is due *only* on the outstanding balance.

You have complete power to pay *more* than the minimum monthly payment and repay the mortgage in *less* time than the specified term. The extent to which you do so is limited only by your resources and ambitions. Even though you take less time and repay more than the minimum, you still satisfy the other two requirements by repaying the entire loan in not more than the specified term and also paying interest on the actual outstanding balance. Nothing more is required.

The door that opens your mortgage to the marvel of prepayment is requirement 4. This is because an amortized mortgage is essentially a simple-interest loan where interest is computed and due only on the *actual* outstanding balance. Mortgage prepayment reduces that balance and thus reduces the amount of interest actually due. As a consequence, any interest that was listed on the schedule, which was based on presumed outstanding balances, is now automatically eliminated. This is why it may be said that "arithmetic takes care of the rest."

As a practical matter, this is how interest is calculated and arithmetic works on the Cliftons' first mortgage payment:

Outstanding Balance	$70,000
Interest Rate	× 11%
Yearly Interest	$ 7,700
Months (divide)	÷ 12
Interest Due	$641.67

This process of calculating interest is repeated every month for which an outstanding loan balance exists. After the interest is calculated it is subtracted from the constant monthly payment, which in our example is $666.63. Whatever is left over from the monthly payment goes to principal ($666.63 − $641.67 = $24.96). Interest is always paid and brought current before any money can be applied to the outstanding loan balance. This includes both normal monthly payments and prepayments. This is true for all mortgage loans, even $70 million loans on commercial office buildings.

You can prove this for yourself by picking any outstanding balance on your personal repayment schedule and performing this process. The interest scheduled for the next payment will be exactly as calculated. You can also see this by inspecting the first 12 months of the Cliftons' amortization schedule.

Table 6

First Year of $70,000 Loan Amortization Schedule: The Cliftons

Scheduled Payment	Interest	Principal	Balance
1	$641.67	$24.96	$69,975.04
2	641.44	25.19	69,949.85
3	641.21	25.42	69,924.43
4	640.97	25.66	69,898.77
5	640.74	25.89	69,872.88
6	640.50	26.13	69,846.75
7	640.26	26.73	69,820.38
8	640.02	26.61	69,793.77
9	639.78	26.85	69,766.92
10	639.53	27.10	69,739,82
11	639.28	27.35	69,712.47
12	639.03	27.60	69,684.87

The first month reflects the same distribution between principal and interest that was shown in the previous calculation. Pick any balance, such as after payment 7, go through the calculation as before, and you will see the interest due on payment 8 will be $640.02. The next calendar month's normal payment will be applied to payment 8, regardless of whether it took the Cliftons seven months or just one month to reduce the balance to that amount. Remember, the repayment schedule is only a presumption; the outstanding balance actually controls the distribution of interest and principal.

Let's follow the arithmetic if the Cliftons make a prepayment of $128.29 on the first month of their schedule. Their normal monthly payment is first applied to payment 1 because all interest must be brought current before principal of any type can be applied. By referring back to the schedule, you can see the first payment reduces the loan balance to $69,975.04. Now their $128.29 prepayment of principal is subtracted directly from the previous loan balance and reduces it to a new balance of $69,846.75. Looking at the schedule again, you can see this is the balance at the end of payment 6. Next month, interest of $640.26 will be due on this new balance. Therefore, the Cliftons' normal payment next month will automatically be applied against payment 7.

Balance		$69,846.74
Interest Rate	×	11%
Yearly Interest		$ 7,683.14
Months (divide)		÷ 12
Interest Due		$640.26

The five payments between payments 2 and 6 have been eliminated from the repayment schedule. The scheduled interest expense never has to be paid. Not only have the Cliftons recaptured five months of the opportunity loss; they have also eliminated $3,204.83 of interest expense.

Table 7

Scheduled Interest		Scheduled Principal
Payment 2	$ 641.44	$ 25.19
3	641.21	25.42
4	640.97	25.66
5	640.74	25.89
6	640.50	26.13
	3,204.86 interest eliminated	128.29 prepayment

This $128.29 is a powerful example of paying yourself first. In addition to building hard-dollar equity, it eliminated $25 of interest expense for every $1 of principal. This dramatic example proves that the timing of prepayments makes a huge difference in results. Furthermore, it's important to note these five payments are eliminated from the front of the repayment schedule, not the back as most people believe. By eliminating payment 2, for instance, the Cliftons eliminated $641.44 of interest expense. If they had eliminated payment 359, they would have eliminated only $11.97 of interest expense. Clearly, eliminating payments from the front of the schedule is extremely important to the effectiveness of a mortgage prepayment strategy. The icing on the cake is that the normal monthly payment begins to acquire more and more purchasing power. Before very long, the additional purchasing power begins to equal the amount of principal accumulated by prepayment.

Mortgage prepayment is a marvelous way to transform your mortgage into an active investment that builds real equity ownership. There are no fancy tricks, no loopholes, no taking advantage of anyone. Just simple arithmetic, arithmetic that's been put to work for you. In the first year alone, assuming the Cliftons prepay $1,802 of principal, they eliminate $33,530 of scheduled interest expense and recapture an extra 53 months, or about four and a half years, of the opportunity loss.

At first it seems hard to believe that your gain isn't made at the lender's expense. After all, someone has to lose for another to gain. Right? Not in this case. That's because the lender still counts its income according to the annual interest rate. All the while you're accelerating principal, you're also paying the interest due on the actual outstanding balance. Therefore, the lender is still earning the proper amount of income on its money. It just so happens that you won't be paying it time and again on virtually the same unchanged balance, and you'll be paying it for 15 years less than others. Don't worry about the lender, though; it will take your accelerated principal and make new mortgage loans, which helps the lender, the new homeowner, and the community.

Despite these impressive results, prepayment doesn't suit everyone's philosophy. For example, the Cliftons have a neighbor by the name of Fred Borden. Fred believes that money invested in the house is essentially idle and therefore prefers to put his money where he thinks it is more active. So let's compare where the Cliftons and Fred stand after year one and year five. They both start with a $70,000 11 percent mortgage. At the end of the first year the Cliftons have jumped 65 payments on the repayment schedule; Fred has moved 12 payments on the schedule. The Cliftons have eliminated more than $33,000 of interest expense; Fred hasn't eliminated any interest and still has an interest obligation of about $169,700. After the fifth and final year the Cliftons have prepaid about $15,000 of principal, jumped 244 payments (more than 20 years), and saved $104,000 of interest expense. It's at this point that the program is completed, and the Cliftons return to paying nothing more than normal monthly payments for the last 10 years of the mortgage. Fred has progressed through the 60 normal payments of a five-year period, reduced his mortgage by a mere $1,985, and still has to work 25 more years to pay about $132,000 more scheduled interest expense.

Fred Borden may not realize it yet, but eliminating unnecessary interest expense is the same as earning money. Of course Fred is earning a solid 8 percent on his $15,000, which was invested elsewhere, but it will amount to only half the nest egg that Don and Arlene will accumulate. And that presumes Fred will leave it untouched for 30 years. One would have to have the patience of St. Thomas Aquinas to not touch this money for 30 years.

Arlene and Don, in contrast, realize that eliminating this interest expense today is the source of their cash nest egg tomorrow. Furthermore, eliminating $33,500 of scheduled interest expense in the first year alone is equivalent to earning a $46,500 salary that is taxed at a 28 percent effective tax rate. Imagine if Arlene uses her part-time telephone answering service income for this purpose. Saving and earning this much money would make her one of the highest-paid homemakers in the country. Her income would be as valuable as Don's full-time salary. The income she earns while staying home with the children is actually buying her family's freedom.

Principal Acceleration Strategy

Principal acceleration is a genuine strategy. It has specific objectives, goals, tactics, timelines, benchmarks, budgets, and tracking methods, all based on the equity perspective. All of these will become clear as we proceed to develop a plan customized to your individual mortgage.

All of these strategic considerations are tied to one core concept—initial gain. That's right. We didn't go through all the trouble of discovering the initial gain on your personal mortgage just to compare the overwhelming amount of opportunity loss. We actually sought that information because it's the key piece of information needed to customize a strategy to your mortgage. In a nutshell, here's why it's the core concept: in exchange for a larger mortgage (initial gain) you traded an extra 15 years of payments (opportunity loss). Now you can reverse that agreement and buy back the 15 years of opportunity loss by paying back the initial gain ahead of schedule. For example, if Don and Arlene Clifton accelerate repayment of their $11,351 initial gain, plus some added money for the cost of time, over the next five years *they'll leapfrog over 15 years of lazy debt and recapture the $230,000 opportunity loss.* Accelerating repayment of the specific amount of principal in the initial gain is also the origin of the term *principal acceleration.*

Just as principal acceleration is distinguished by its strategic connection to the initial gain, so are all of its planning criteria. Here's a sample of these planning criteria:

Objective:	Recapture all 15 years of the opportunity loss.
Goal:	Start building equity ownership today.
Tactic:	Eliminate lazy debt.
Budget:	Initial gain divided into monthly/yearly amounts.
Tracking:	Conform to original amortization schedule.
Benchmark:	Completion by the two-for-one point.
Timetable:	Five-year plan.

These criteria become the strategy dog that wags the prepayment tail. The last two criteria deserve immediate attention; we'll explore these now. The importance of the remaining criteria will become quite evident as we go along.

Five-Year Program

There's only a limited amount of time to repay the initial gain before it becomes too late to recapture all 15 years of the opportunity loss. One reason is numerical; the other is affordability. First, as a general rule, all acceleration should be completed prior to reaching approximately payment 240 in the repayment schedule. As another general rule, payment 240 is the beginning of the equity zone. Technically, the point of completion should be where the schedule calls for $2 of interest for every $1 of principal. The two-for-one point is an arithmetic crossover point where the cost of recapturing payments begins to skyrocket and the amount of eliminated interest dwindles. The actual two-for-one point shifts according to the interest rate. It's earlier for lower interest rates and later for higher interest rates. Sometimes you can go up to the actual 50-50 point with some measure of success, but not further. As a practical matter, whatever is accomplished by the time the two-for-one point is reached is usually all that is ever accomplished. To succeed in eliminating 180 payments (15 years of opportunity loss) prior to payment 240, you have only 60 payments (240 − 180) or *5 calendar years* to accomplish your mission.

Be careful not to confuse calendar months with schedule payments. *Months* refer to real calendar time, while *payments* refer to artificial scheduled time. Thus scheduled payment 60 may not be the 60th month of payments if you are accelerating principal. Payment 60 may, in fact, occur in the 12th month of payments. This distinction will prove helpful later, when we describe how to accelerate your principal.

Affordability is the other reason that five years is the

Figure 3

Average Price to Eliminate One Payment: The Cliftons

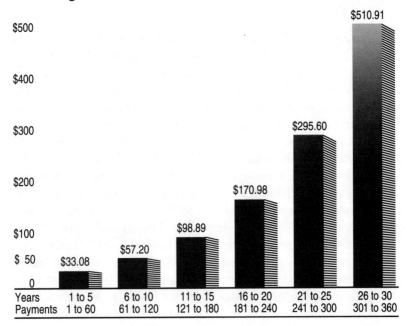

ideal length of time and the two-for-one point is the ideal point to quit. The price to eliminate a single mortgage payment becomes so high it's simply not affordable. As Figure 3 demonstrates for the Cliftons' $70,000 11 percent mortgage, payable at $666.63 per month, the cost of eliminating a single month from the amortization schedule starts at an affordable $33 and ends at a prohibitive $510.

During the first five years the average principal prepayment is only $33 to eliminate one mortgage payment worth $666. This relationship corresponds to the previous savings-to-cost ratio of about $19 to $1. Now notice what happens with each succeeding 5-year period. It increases by almost three-fourths with each period. By the fourth period the cost has increased more than fivefold to $170 and is on the threshold of becoming too expensive. Beyond this point, the end of the 20th year or payment 240, the cost outweighs the benefits, and the program should be completed.

Principal acceleration recognizes the need to be finished by payment 240. Furthermore, it acknowledges the merit of eliminating payments while they're still cheap, so it eliminates a multiple number of payments in the earliest periods. For instance, $100 prepaid against the first period of the Cliftons' mortgage nets a savings of about $1,898. If they wait until the last period, however, their $100 will buy less than one-fifth of one payment, a net savings of about $30. This is a shocking difference, yet it is merely the difference between the front and back of the mortgage coming into play. Eliminating a multiple number of payments when they are cheap is a tactic that will be covered more completely later.

This race between time and affordability is the reason a 5-year strategy is needed to accelerate the initial gain successfully. Just be certain you're sure of the timing, which is worth reviewing: The overall objective is to repay 20 years, or 240 scheduled payments, of lazy debt in only 5 years of actual payments. Of these 20 years, 15 years of payments are eliminated by principal acceleration, while the other 5 years are repaid with normal mortgage payments. Both prepayment and normal repayment are made concurrently during those 5 years. Upon concluding the program at scheduled payment 240, acceleration ceases. Only 10 years of payments remain, all of which are preserved for normal monthly payments because their purchasing power works hard to build real equity ownership. The net result is 5 years of principal acceleration, 10 years of normal payments, and 15 years of liberated payments that are devoted to your nest egg. You've succeeded in getting rid of the worst parts of a 30-year mortgage and keeping the best.

Accelerating the Initial Gain

It matters little whether you accelerate repayment of the initial gain in monthly, quarterly, or yearly increments or in one lump sum. The results will be largely the same. That's not the constraint. The biggest constraint is the amount of available money. It's certainly not recommended that you spend your last dime pursuing a principal acceleration program. Principal acceleration is intended to be in addition to and a balance with adequate savings, good insurance coverage, pension plans, and stocks and bonds, for instance. There's only so much money, however. Naturally there are budget constraints. The purpose of this section is to provide you with the basic five-year principal acceleration plan, which forms the foundation on which to build variations that fit your resources and ambitions.

The basic principal acceleration plan averages the initial gain, plus a bit extra for the cost of repaying it over time, over a 60-month period and accelerates this amount of principal every month. In the case of Don and Arlene, their initial gain is $11,351. Since they are repaying it over a 5-year period at an 11 percent annual rate, however, an extra $3,470 must be added to account for this time. (I'll tell you how this was calculated in the coffee break.) Hence the total amount of principal acceleration is $14,821. The average amount of principal acceleration over that 60-calendar-month period is $247 per month. Accelerate this amount, and arithmetic takes care of the rest; it eliminates lazy debt, recaptures all 15 years of the opportunity loss, and positions the Cliftons at the beginning of the blue zone, where 50 percent of their monthly payments starts being credited to principal. Their mortgage is now smart, hardworking debt.

One variation is to make quarterly payments of $741 each. Similarly, you could make lump sum payments every year instead of monthly or quarterly. The lump sum payment would be $2,964. Or you could combine lower monthly accelerations and periodic lump sum payments to bring the average up to desired levels. There are slight differences in effect among the various schedules, but they are immaterial. You could even pay it off in one fell swoop if the resources were available.

A perennial question is whether it's too late for the Cliftons if they are already five years into their mortgage. This is where the distinction between calendar months and scheduled payments comes into play. Although they may be five years into their mortgage, they are still only 60 scheduled payments into it. This means there's still a lot of opportunity to eliminate interest expense and recapture large chunks of the opportunity loss before hitting the two-for-one point located at approximately payment 240. Depending on their ambitions or other considerations, such as retirement or college tuition, they may choose to accelerate past the two-for-one point and go up to the one-for-one point. Modifications such as these are relatively simple now that you know how to tie your strategy to the initial gain. If, for example, you're on payment 36 and still intend to eliminate 15 years or 180 payments, you can arrive at a new initial gain by subtracting the balance at payment 144 (180

− 36) from the balance at payment 324 (360 − 36). Then you can see if it's possible to average this modified initial gain over 60 months without going beyond the one-for-one point. Perhaps it will be necessary to create a 4½-year rather than a 5-year plan. Whatever the individual situation, you're now empowered to create a plan that yields the results you desire.

Speaking of that, it's time for a coffee break, where, in addition to stretching your legs, you will learn how to discover the ideal amount of monthly principal acceleration for your personal mortgage.

Coffee Break

"Arithmetic doesn't lie." You've often heard that phrase, but what does it mean? We know statistics can be moved around to prove whatever point is necessary. Yet the same cannot be said about arithmetic. It is completely honest because it's entirely consistent and nothing in its theory contradicts any other part of its theory. No calculation opposes any other calculation. No answer lacks agreement with another answer. It's all tied together in a perfectly unified system.

To demonstrate this point, here's an arithmetic riddle where the same answer will always result: Pick any number from 1 to 10. Double that amount, add 4 to the new amount, divide that amount in half, and now subtract your original number from the last amount. The answer is given on the last line of this coffee break. Don't peek!

That riddle was just for fun. The real exercise is directed at discovering the average and ideal amount of principal acceleration for your mortgage. The first step, of course, is to know the initial gain on your individual mortgage. If you didn't do it before, now's the time to go back to learn this amount. The second step involves mortgage tables that tell you the precise amount of monthly acceleration.

Standard mortgage tables are available in almost every bookstore. All mortgage lenders keep one in their top drawer, if it's not already programmed into a handheld computer. As a matter of fact, you could probably telephone one of these friendly professionals and get the answer in a matter of seconds. Doing it yourself, though, gives you the confidence of knowing why it's the right answer. Table 8 is a sample of the monthly payments necessary to amortize an 11 percent loan. A mortgage table includes one column for every year—I've listed only three columns for this example.

Table 8

**Monthly Payments Required to Repay Principal:
11 Percent Loan**

Amount	5 Years	7 Years	10 Years
$ 1,000	$ 21.75	$ 17.13	$ 13.78
5,000	108.72	85.62	68.88
10,000	217.43	171.23	137.76
11,000	239.17	188.35	151.53
12,000	260.91	206.12	165.31

To get the average amount of principal acceleration on the Cliftons' initial gain of $11,351, they first go down the amount column until they locate the two closest amounts, $11,000 and $12,000. Next they go to the proper years column, 5 years. Then they go down that column until the two points intersect. In this case the exact point is somewhere between $239.17 and $260.91. They interpolate the precise amount by taking .351 of the difference between the two amounts. The precise answer is $246.80. Rounded up to the next dollar, the average budget is $247. Accelerating by $247 each month for 60 months gives us a total of $14,820, which accounts for the additional $3,470 over the $11,351 initial gain that was noted earlier.

When you perform this exercise on your initial gain, don't forget to refer to the right page for *your* interest rate.

By the way, the answer to the riddle is 2. It's always 2, no matter what number you picked between 1 and 10.

End of Break

You may have noticed one hitch to this average approach of accelerating the initial gain—it's often more expensive than many homeowners can afford. If you haven't noticed this hurdle, then it probably isn't a problem. Most people, though, have less money shortly after buying a home than they'll enjoy later, as their income grows and other debts are paid off. Consequently they usually can't afford a 30 percent increase over their normal P&I payment, which nets to 20 percent or so over their PITI (principal, interest, taxes, and insurance) payment. There are a couple of solutions to this dilemma. One solution is to repay the initial gain over a longer period of time. The other solution is to lower the monthly average in the first half of the program and increase it in the second half, thereby giving you time to catch up.

The first solution entails accelerating the initial gain over a 7-year period instead of the flagship 5-year approach. Accelerating it over 2 additional years results in a 20 percent reduction in the average monthly amount. The name of this approach is the extended plan. The process is exactly the same as previously, except the Cliftons use the 7 year column. Interpolating between $188.35 and $206.12, they arrive at $194.59. Rounding it up to the next dollar, the extended budget is $195, which is about $50 less than for the 5-year plan. There's a trade-off for this lower budget, however: they won't recapture all 15 years of the opportunity loss prior to hitting the two-for-one point. They will miss it by approximately 20 percent. This is a regrettable loss but one that may be necessary.

The other solution is to lower the monthly average in the first half of the program and increase it in the second half. There are several benefits to this approach. Foremost, it enables you to get started when you couldn't otherwise afford it. It makes your program substantially more affordable in the early years, when you need it most, as well as provides time to increase your income, pay the cost of drapes, decorating, appliances, landscaping, and so forth and also pay off other installment debts. It further provides a tracking method that allows you to monitor the lender's proper application of accelerated principal, which also provides an easy way to rectify a problem if mistakes do occur. The name of this solution is the "Custom Cunningham Plan."

Because the Cunningham Plan has been practiced for a number of years prior to the publication of this book, it has acquired a number of synonyms along the way. One of them is the Custom Prepayment Plan; another is the Cunningham Prepayment Plan. There may be one or two others as well. Whenever you encounter these names in the material, be assured that it is the same principal acceleration strategy we have been discussing.

Custom Cunningham Plan. Although the average approach to accelerating the initial gain is guaranteed to succeed, and the most simple to learn and implement, an average of $247 per month is nevertheless too rich for the Cliftons. The alternative is to lower it in the first half of the program and increase it in the second half.

The graph in Figure 4 shows how the average principal acceleration budget is positioned at scheduled payment 120, which is the halfway point between payments 1 and 240.

Figure 4

Average Budget

Constant Amount   **$247**

| 1 | 30 | 60 | 90 | 120 | 150 | 180 | 210 | 240 |

Scheduled Payments

Instead of paying a constant average of $247 we now divide the repayment schedule into these eight increments, one increment every 30 scheduled payments. Those increments situated prior to payment 120 will be lower than $247, and those after payment 120 will be higher. This means there is a starting budget and then three adjustments before hitting the average of $247 at payment 120, and another three budget adjustments after reaching the average amount.

The budget starts at payment 1 with $129, which is almost 50 percent less than the average of $247. It also reduced principal acceleration to a 19 percent increase over the P&I payment and probably about 12 percent over the PITI payment. This is substantially less than the average and within the affordability range of most homeowners. Each 30 scheduled payments (not months), the budget is increased by $29 per month. Actually, the exact amount is $29.35, which accounts for the slight rounding differences shown in Figure 5—Don and Arlene's budget for their entire principal acceleration program.

Figure 5

Cunningham Plan

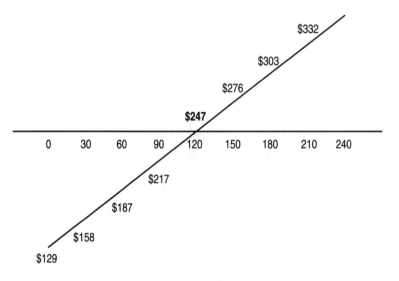

Although this approach allows most people to get started, some people aren't happy with the increases in the second half. Even though they don't come up for a couple of years, some people won't even start the program because of them. It seems to be just another excuse for sticking to the old debt strategy. Refusing to take a step today for fear of needing to take another later reminds me of another of Aesop's fables. This is the story of "The Two Frogs": "One hot summer, the lake in which two frogs lived was completely dried up, and they were obliged to set off in search of water elsewhere. Coming to a deep and delicious cool well, one of the frogs proposed that they jump in at once. 'Wait a bit,' cried the other; 'if that should dry up, how could we get out again?'"

A $203 increase from $129 to $332 seems like a big jump, but you must remember that it happens over a five-year period. It's probable that a family earning over $40,000 per year will increase its income by over $200 a month over the same five years. There's inflation to consider and a range of other factors that will help cash-flow the cost of these increases. Moreover, it should be noted that these increases aren't a function of the Cunningham Plan per se but of the increasing cost to eliminate a single mortgage payment at the back end of the repayment schedule. This increase is unavoidable. The only question is how to eliminate enough payments before reaching the "wall."

Obviously these graphs are only a preview of how to customize a Cunningham Plan for your personal mortgage. Like consulting a road map prior to starting off on a vacation, it helps to know where you're going before you get on the highway. The next chapter, "Your Ideal Budget," tells you how to determine your ideal starting budget and the adjustments necessary to keep pace with the cost of eliminating payments.

A Last Word and Heading On . . .

A twelfth month after Algamish had gone he again returned and said to Arkad, "Son, have you paid to yourself not less than one-tenth of all you have earned for the past year?"

I answered proudly, "Yes, master, I have."

"That is good," he answered beaming upon me, "and what have you done with it?"

"I have given it to Azmur, the brickmaker, who told me he was traveling over the far seas and in Tyre he would buy for me the rare jewels of the Phoenicians. When he returns we shall sell these at high prices and divide the earnings."

"Every fool must learn," he growled, "but why trust the knowledge of a brickmaker about jewels? . . . Your savings are gone, youth, you have jerked your wealth-tree up by the roots. But plant another. Try again. And next time if you would have advice about jewels, go to the jewel merchant.

If you would know the truth about sheep, go to the herdsman. . . ." Saying this he went away.

Again, twelve months later, Algamish came to the room of the scribes and addressed me. "What progress have you made since I last saw you?"

"I have paid myself faithfully," I replied, "and my savings I have entrusted to Agger the shield-maker, to buy bronze, and each fourth month he does pay me the rental."

"That is good. And what do you do with the rental?"

"I do have a great feast. . . ."

To which Algamish laughed, "You do eat the children of your savings. Then how do you expect them to work for you? . . ."

Nor did I again see Algamish for two years. . . . And he said to me, "Arkad, hast thou yet achieved the wealth thou dreamed of?"

And I answered, "Not yet all that I desire, but some I have and it earns more, and its earnings earn even more."

"And do you still take the advice of brickmakers?"

"About brickmaking they give good advice," I retorted.

"Arkad," he continued, "you have learned your lessons well. You first learned to live upon less than you could earn. Next you learned to seek advice from those who were competent through their own experiences to give it. And, lastly, you have learned to make gold work for you."

Note: Not surprisingly, Arkad went on to become the richest man in Babylon and a great teacher. The Seven Cures for a Lean Purse was his most famous lesson. These cures are not just for an ancient time; money is governed today by the same laws that controlled it when prosperous men thronged the streets of Babylon 6,000 years ago.

5
Your Ideal Budget

N ow we move into the implementation stage of principal acceleration. This is the part that some people hate (fear) and others love. The mere thought of numbers makes some people's eyes glaze over. Others' eyes blaze with anticipation as their fingers twitch nervously at their HP calculators. But hey! It's just not that difficult. It may be a little involved, but it's not complex. There may be a few tricks, but there are no mysteries. We'll cover this material in a way that will make everyone happy. It will be plain enough to the people who hate arithmetic yet substantial enough for the HP calculator crowd to get their money's worth.

This chapter has only two objectives. First it will explain how you can find the monthly principal acceleration budget that's ideal for your personal mortgage. *Ideal* in this context means one that's affordable yet powerful enough to eliminate the lazy-debt portion of your mortgage and recapture the full opportunity loss. Second, it will teach you how to make periodic adjustments to your starting ideal budget so it keeps pace with the increasing price to eliminate scheduled mortgage payments.

Up to this point we have only discussed 30-year mortgages. You might be wondering how these monthly budgets and periodic adjustments affect a 15-year mortgage as well as adjustable-rate mortgages. Adjustable-rate mortgages are especially affected by these budget and adjustment considerations, which will be addressed in the last section of this chapter, "ARMs Control." Fifteen-year mortgages are not affected by these budget and adjustment considerations, though, because an entirely different strategy of principal acceleration is recommended for these shorter-term mortgages.

Accelerating a 15-Year Mortgage

Fifteen-year mortgages are becoming more popular as people take advantage of lower interest rates and refinance into mortgages with shorter terms. Some people want to do even better and are interested in shortening the term even further, perhaps even owning the home free and clear of all encumbrances in 10 years or so. What's the best way to do that?

There are several considerations that make a 15-year mortgage different from a 30-year one. Overall the biggest difference is that the change in true cost (Figure 2) in the three zones of a 15-year mortgage is not nearly as dramatic as the change in the first three zones of a 30-year mortgage. The graph is far flatter in a 15-year mortgage. Accordingly, a strategic principal acceleration plan will not make that much difference over a conventional mortgage prepayment method. All things considered, the program that's most affordable and easiest to implement is the best approach.

In brief, presuming the objective is to eliminate 5 years of mortgage payments, the best way to prepay a 15-year mortgage is to repay it with the monthly principal and interest payments of a 10-year mortgage. There are several advantages to this simple method. First, it's easy to implement because it is a constant payment every month for 10 years. For example, if Don and Arlene had a 15-year term on their $70,000 11 percent mortgage, their monthly P&I payment would be $795.62. If they choose to pay it off on a 10-year schedule, though, their new constant payment would be $964.25. Each month they would write the check for this higher amount.

The second, and perhaps most important, advantage is affordability. The increase in monthly payments between a 10-year and 15-year principal acceleration schedule is $168.63 per month, which is about a 21 percent increase. At first blush a 21 percent increase may seem large, but it's not when seen in the context of $168.63 and when compared to other methods. An initial gain approach requires you to eliminate 5 years of payments prior to hitting the 50-50 point, which means the monthly payment would have to be increased up to 50 percent or so for a period of three years. This is simply too high. Other conventional methods, such as the biweekly or next-month method, either would fail to recapture 5 years of payments or would become so expensive that they would be abandoned prior to completion.

The third advantage of this 10-year constant approach is that it eliminates about 40 percent of the scheduled interest expense. The 15-year schedule calls for $73,211 of interest expense, while the 10-year schedule calls for $45,710. Equally important, it adds another 5 years of capital and earnings to your nest egg. This additional time will often double the size of your nest egg. Quite a good reward, don't you agree?

If this constant approach is so good, you might ask why you shouldn't simply repay a 30-year mortgage according to the schedule of a 15-year mortgage and avoid figuring all this initial gain stuff. There are a number of reasons why it doesn't work on a 30-year mortgage. First is the practical, human-nature aspect. The average time that people stay in one home is about 6 years. So successful programs are completed in about 5 years or so. Besides, few people have the perseverance to pursue a program for 15 years. Moreover, since the dynamics of a 30-year mortgage are so different from those of a 15-year one, the results of this constant method are substantially less than the initial gain strategy, which really attacks the front of the mortgage, where most of the interest expense is located. Furthermore, it preserves the equity zone for normal mortgage payments, which are doing most of the work anyway.

Recommending different remedies for different mortgages doesn't reflect on the effectiveness of the Cunningham Plan; it simply means that we're not committed to a particular technique. Results are the only measure of our commitment.

For those of you with a 30-year mortgage who find that accelerating an average amount of principal is unaffordable, there is the solution of the Cunningham Plan. It lowers the amount of acceleration in the first half of the program and increases it in the second half. The first step in constructing such a strategy is to customize an ideal acceleration budget to the particulars of your personal mortgage.

Three Ways to Determine Your Ideal Budget

There are three shortcuts to learning the ideal starting budget for your mortgage:

1. amortization schedule
2. conversion table
3. standard mortgage tables

Amortization Schedule

The amortization schedule is the most direct method of learning the proper budget. Recognizing that the amortization schedule is a precise accounting of your mortgage, you shouldn't be surprised that the ideal budget amount lies hidden somewhere in that forest of information. This is how to find it. First, read down the amortization schedule until you reach scheduled payment 180 (the 15th year). Next, seek out the principal associated with the very next number (payment 181), and presto! You've just found the right amount for your initial budget. In general the ideal budget corresponds to payment 181 because it is the amount of credit for principal loan reduction that your normal mortgage payment would have received if you had started with a 15-year rather than a 30-year mortgage. Thus, if you wish to eliminate the extra 15 years of mortgage payments, you should start prepaying the principal associated with those 15 years.

The reason we chose the 15th year is that our objective is to eliminate 15 years from the 30-year repayment schedule. We wish to eliminate a full 15 years because earning compound interest for 15 years creates a next egg that is twice as big as earning interest for only 10 years. Furthermore, starting with this budget lets you complete the entire program and reach payment 240 in only five years. This is true even if you're starting the program late.

Let's use the Cliftons' mortgage as an example and find the ideal budget amount for their mortgage. The following table is the applicable portion of the amortization schedule for their 11 percent $70,000 30-year mortgage.

Table 9

Amortization Schedule: The Cliftons

Payment	Interest	Principal	Balance
178	$541.10	$125.53	$58,904.07
179	539.95	126.68	58,777.39
180	538.79	127.84	58,649.55
181	537.62	129.01	58,520.54

Since the Cliftons want to eliminate 15 years of mortgage payments, they first locate payment 180. Next they locate the principal scheduled at payment 181, which is $129.01. This is their ideal budget. This means that in addition to their normal monthly payment of $666.63, they will make a principal acceleration of approximately $129 a month. Note the word *approximate*. They have the choice of paying a constant $129 per month for a prescribed time period or accelerating by an amount closest to $129 that conforms to the principal listed on the repayment schedule. For example, if you refer to the Cliftons' repayment schedule (Table 7) in the previous chapter, the exact total of principal payments 2–6 is $128.29. Therefore, $128.29 is the exact amount they could prepay during the first month of their mortgage. The value of such a precise approach is that you can always check on the proper application of your monies. Staying on the original repayment schedule allows the lender's ending balance to be checked against your records of the correct balance after principal accelerations. Mistakes are easily corrected when both you and the lender are working from the same road map. The effectiveness of the program is about the same regardless of whether you choose the simpler constant approach or the sticking-to-the-schedule approach. For example purposes, and because it's the best tracking system, we will use the precise method.

If you don't have an amortization schedule and you can't order one for about $10 from a nearby bank, real estate office, accountant, or financial planner, the next alternative is a conversion table.

Conversion Table

Multiplying your principal and interest payment by the appropriate factor in the conversion table will also provide the correct starting budget. That's because I prepared it from the appropriate repayment schedules. This is how it works. Find the interest rate of your mortgage and then note the factor alongside it. Simply multiply your principal and interest payment (eliminate taxes, hazard and mortgage insurance, and so forth) by this factor, and the result is your ideal principal acceleration budget.

Only the conversion table should be used if your mortgage interest rate is lower than 10 percent. As interest rates drop below 10 percent, the dynamics of the amortization schedule change a bit. Therefore, it's necessary to make some corrections to account for these changed dynamics. Rather than provide specific instructions in each of the three methods, I chose instead to consolidate this modification in only the conversion table. The factors in this table incorporate these corrections.

Table 10

Conversion Table

Mortgage Rate	Factor	Mortgage Rate	Factor
12.00	.1668	8.75	.3196
11.75	.1731	8.50	.3349
11.50	.1796	8.25	.3529
11.25	.1864	8.00	.3691
11.00	.1934	7.75	.3893
10.75	.2063	7.50	.4052
10.50	.2217	7.25	.4251
10.25	.2316	7.00	.4430
10.00	.2439	6.75	.4637
9.75	.2589	6.50	.4823
9.50	.2722	6.25	.5037
9.25	.2882	6.00	.5229
9.00	.3026		

This is how the Cliftons used the table to determine their budget. First, they found the factor corresponding to their 11 percent mortgage, which turned out to be .1934. Next, they multiplied their principal and interest payment of $666.63 by .1934; the result is $128.93. As it happens, the conversion table method is $.08 off the amortization schedule, but the difference is immaterial. Similarly, if your interest rate falls between two rates listed on this table, you will have to interpolate between the two, which may introduce other rounding differences. Don't worry about either situation, because the success of your program depends on moving in harmony with the changing nature of your mortgage, not down-to-the-penny accuracy.

Standard Mortgage Tables

The final method calls for referring to standard mortgage tables. This is a more involved method and requires that you recall the initial gain in borrowing power acquired for taking a 30-year mortgage instead of a 15-year one that you learned in the last chapter.

Standard mortgage tables are available in almost every bookstore. The following matrix is a sample page for an 11 percent mortgage.

Table 11

11 Percent Mortgage Table
Monthly Payments Required to Repay Principal

Amount	5 Years	10 Years	15 Years	20 Years
$ 1,000	$ 21.75	$ 13.78	$ 11.37	$ 10.33
5,000	108.72	68.88	56.83	51.61
10,000	217.43	137.76	113.66	103.22
11,000	239.17	151.53	125.03	113.55
12,000	260.91	165.31	136.40	123.87

Each page of the mortgage table is referenced by its interest rate, therefore the first step is to find the appropriate interest rate. Now, glancing at the abbreviated table, you will see it is organized into rows and columns. Rows are read from left to right, and columns are read from top to bottom. Starting at the left, the column under the "Amount" heading shows the increase in borrowing power (initial gain). In this example the amounts range from $1,000 to $12,000. In the real books they range from $25,000 to $100,000. In the case of the Cliftons the increase or initial gain is $11,351. The other columns are headed by different periods of time listed over each column. In this example, they range from only 5 years to 20 years. In real life they usually range from 1 year to 40 years. These time periods refer to the length of time chosen to repay the principal or initial gain in the "Amount" column. Below each column are dollar amounts. These are the monthly amounts that must be paid to retire the initial gain listed in the "Amount" column within the chosen time period. For example, is you wish to repay $5,000 over a 10-year period, your payments will be $68.88 per month. Still with me? As I mentioned at the outset, it may be involved, but it's not complicated.

The Cliftons could have arrived at the same budget they discovered in the amortization schedule by simply researching the appropriate page in the mortgage tables. The increase in the size of their mortgage for taking a 30-year mortgage is $11,351. Therefore, they go down the "Amount" column until they reach the amount closest to the initial gain. In this case it is the $11,000 point. Now they go across to the 15-year column, which is the number of years added to the repayment schedule for borrowing the initial gain amount and the number of years that they now wish to eliminate. The intersecting amount is $125.03. This is fairly close to their actual budget, but not exactly. If the

Cliftons want to arrive at the exact amount, they need to prorate the difference between the $11,000 initial gain and the $12,000 upgrade. Since their actual upgrade is $351 off the $11,000 amount, they would take .351 of the difference between $125.03 and $136.40. So they multiply this difference of $11.37 by .351 for an additional budget amount of $3.99. Add this amount back to the $125.03, and the Cliftons' ideal principal acceleration budget comes out at $129.02, only a single penny off the amortization method. Though they give the same results, the mortgage tables are unquestionably the most involved method of learning your ideal budget.

Whether you choose the mortgage tables, amortization schedule, or conversion tables is entirely a matter of your personal preference. The amortization schedule leads straight to the ideal budget. If you don't have an amortization schedule, the conversion table is a good alternative. Standard mortgage tables locate the ideal budget by referring back to the original mortgage upgrade. All these methods work equally well. However, methodology isn't the critical factor. Eliminating 15 years of mortgage payments and saving the majority of interest expense is the critical objective.

A principal acceleration budget that's ideal for your individual mortgage will accomplish these objectives. You don't need to know why it works; just prepay the right amount, and you can be assured that arithmetic takes care of the rest. This budget prepays an amount that is guaranteed to complete the entire program by the benchmark at payment 240 and without going beyond the point where one-third of the original loan balance is repaid. By virtue of completing the program by these benchmarks, you maximize your savings and eliminate the greatest number of mortgage payments. The custom principal acceleration plan is guaranteed to succeed.

Coffee Break

This is an opportunity for you to discover the ideal budget for your own mortgage. Remember, the foremost purpose of a budget is to account for the changing nature of your mortgage and achieve your objectives before hitting the 2-for-1 point, which is also about when one-third of the balance has been repaid.

The first step in learning the proper budget for your mortgage is to refer to the mortgage tables, your amortization schedule, or the handy conversion table. If you're using the amortization schedule, first locate payment 180. Don't worry if you're starting the program somewhere in mid-schedule. You should still locate payment 180, for it serves as the benchmark for all budgets. Next, locate the principal associated with the very next payment—the ideal amount with which to initiate your equity budget.

Method I: Amortization Schedule

Principal scheduled for payment 181 = $_____

If you're using the conversion chart, simply multiply your normal principal and interest payment by the appropriate factor; the result is your initial budget.

Method II: Conversion Table

Monthly payment $_____ × _____ factor

= $_____

If you refer to mortgage tables, first learn the amount of your mortgage upgrade (initial gain; you calculated this on page 75). Then search under the appropriate year column (15 years) for the monthly budget that relates to the principal upgrade (initial gain) amount.

Method III: Mortgage Tables

Principal Upgrade $_____

Amortized over 15 years = $_____

Take your time and enjoy your break. There's no need to rush through this exercise. Sleep on it overnight if you wish. The only important consideration is learning the budget that compensates for the changes in the true cost of your mortgage.

 *End of Break*

Nothing stays the same, not even your fixed mortgage. That's why you need a principal acceleration plan that changes along with changes in your mortgage.

The next section shows you how to adjust your initial budget periodically to keep moving in harmony with the repayment schedule. Following this short discussion, we begin to explore a month-by-month example of implementing the Cliftons' custom principal acceleration plan. The combination of starting with the ideal budget and adjusting it to stay in harmony with your mortgage is undoubtedly the best way to unscramble your nest egg.

You've probably noticed that I've frequently used the

word *initial* or *beginning* in connection with the principal acceleration budget. The reason for these qualifiers is that nothing is immune to the constant process of change, not even the ideal budget for your mortgage. It too must evolve and change so as to continue operating in harmony with the dynamics of your repayment schedule.

As you now know, your results decline and the price of principal acceleration increases as you proceed through the repayment schedule. If your initial budget was unchanged, it would eliminate fewer and fewer payments until it became impossible to eliminate all 15 years of mortgage payments before hitting the wall at payment 240. Therefore, periodic budget adjustments are necessary. These adjustments are the second half of a custom principal acceleration plan that's designed to fit the dynamics of your personal repayment schedule.

The first section is devoted to discovering the perfect adjustment for your initial budget. The second section is devoted to learning how to modify your initial budget in the event the principal acceleration budget is more than your finances allow. The name of this latter modification is the extended plan. The extended plan is especially good for mortgages lower that 9.5 percent or so, because the lower the interest rate, the higher the monthly principal acceleration budget.

Timely Adjustments

Table 12 was drawn from the Cliftons' mortgage and shows the steady increase in the average cost to eliminate a single mortgage payment.

As you've seen previously, the average cost to eliminate a single payment goes up about 73 percent with each successive five-year period on an 11 percent mortgage. Conversely, savings suffer a steady decline.

This table presents a loud and clear message: unless the Cliftons make adjustments to their initial budget of $129, it

Table 12

Average Cost and Savings of Principal Acceleration: The Cliftons

Payment No.	Average Principal Acceleration	Average Savings
1–60	$ 33.08	$633.55
61–120	57.20	609.43
121–180	98.89	567.74
181–240	170.98	495.65
241–300	295.60	371.03
310–360	510.91	155.52

will eliminate fewer payments and save less money until they are forced to quit at payment 240 without having eliminated 15 years of payments. It's like a footrace. The initial budget gives you a head start, and the race begins with your taking a commanding lead, saving four or five payments with every principal acceleration. But as you move steadily down the course, the pack starts to catch up. If you're going to reach the finish line before the rest, you'll have to make strategic adjustments along the way. The most important of these is to accelerate your pace. In this case that means increasing your principal acceleration budget.

The initial budget must compensate for the increasing cost to eliminate mortgage payments. But by how *much* should the budget be adjusted? And not only by how much but *when* should it be adjusted?

How Much?

There isn't a single answer to this question, because the actual adjustment varies according to its interest rate. In general, the higher the interest rate, the less principal there is in each mortgage payment, and therefore the smaller the amount of the adjustment. Conversely, the lower the interest rate, the more principal in each payment, and the higher the amount needed to keep pace. Fortunately, the amount of the adjustment is easy to learn, and once determined it remains the same for the entire life of the principal acceleration plan.

The amount of your budget adjustment is determined by an adjustment factor. There is a different factor for each interest rate. And, as before, corrections for low interest rates have been incorporated. As with the shortcuts to learning your initial budget, you'll simply have to trust that my arithmetic is correct. There will be plenty of time later to verify its accuracy.

Table 13

Budget Adjustment Factors

Interest Rate	Factor	Interest Rate	Factor
12.00	.2125	8.75	.2100
11.75	.2150	8.50	.2100
11.50	.2200	8.25	.2075
11.25	.2225	8.00	.2075
11.00	.2275	7.75	.2050
10.75	.2325	7.50	.2050
10.50	.2375	7.25	.2025
10.25	.2350	7.00	.2025
10.00	.2300	6.75	.2000
9.75	.2250	6.50	.2000
9.50	.2225	6.25	.1975
9.25	.2150	6.00	.1975
9.00	.2125		

Here is how to use the budget adjustment factors (Table 13). Simply multiply your initial budget by the appropriate factor, and you've discovered the adjustment that's ideal for your mortgage. Someone with an 11 percent mortgage, such as the Cliftons, should adjust the budget by a factor of .2275. After they multiply their $129 budget by .2275, they arrive at a constant adjustment amount of $29.35.

Budget ___$129___ × Factor ___.2275___ = ___$29.35___

Another person with a hypothetical budget of $65 and a 10 percent mortgage should adjust it by .2300 for a constant dollar adjustment of $14.95.

Budget ___$65___ × Factor ___.2300___ = ___$14.95___

Whenever it's time to adjust the budget, it is adjusted by the *same dollar amount*. For example, the first time the Cliftons' budget is adjusted, it increases from $129 to $158. The second time it is adjusted, it increases by the same $29 to a new budget of $187. Likewise, the person with a 10 percent mortgage adjusts his or her mortgage by $14.95 every time an adjustment is required.

As a practical matter, the factors in this chart have been rounded up or down to the next even ¼ percent with the result that the adjustment is pennies off the pinpoint accurate adjustment. Fortunately, this rounding process doesn't affect the success of the program.

When?

When the budget should be adjusted is the next question. In short, the answer is that the initial budget should be adjusted *every 30 scheduled payments*. Adjusting the budget every 30 scheduled payments serves two purposes. First, it keeps pace with the progressive cost to eliminate mortgage payments. Second, it paces the adjustments evenly between scheduled payment 30 and payment 240. The symmetry of these adjustments matches the symmetry of the original mortgage.

Notice that the adjustment is made every 30 *scheduled* payments and not every 30 calendar, or real, months. *Schedule* time refers to the original repayment schedule, which is not the same thing as real or calendar time. Real time is the 12 months between December of last year and December of this year. In contrast, schedule time is the *assumption* of how many months you would take to repay X amount of money. For instance, the schedule assumes you need 60 months to make 60 payments' worth of principal loan reduction. In fact it may require only 11 calendar months to repay 60 scheduled payments' worth of principal. Schedule time and calendar time may, therefore, be very different. To avoid confusion in the ensuing discussion, I will refer to schedule time as *payments* and real, or calendar, time as *months*. An example of such a reference would be that the Cliftons paid off 65 payments in only 12 months.

Let's return to the Cliftons' mortgage to create a schedule of adjustments. We've already determined that their initial budget is approximately $129 a month, that the appropriate adjustment factor is .2275, and that thus the constant adjustment amount is $29 every 30 scheduled payments. Table 14 summarizes the adjustments to the Cliftons' budget from payment 1 through payment 240.

Table 14

Adjustment Table: The Cliftons

Payment No.	Increase	Budget
0–30	$ 0	$129
31–60	29	158
61–90	29	187
91–120	29	216
121–150	29	245
151–180	29	274
181–210	29	303
211–240	29	332

The adjustment table works well for the Cliftons. Besides being an excellent planning tool, it allows them to start principal accelerations at a lower amount and fund future budget increases out of future income. For instance, to qualify for a $70,000 11 percent mortgage, the Cliftons probably earn more than $35,000 per year. Earning no more than 2 percent pay increases per year means they'll increase their income by $700 in the first year alone. This is about $58 a month, which is far more than the budget increase of $29 per month and indicates that budget increases are less an obstacle than they appear at first blush. Who knows? Perhaps in five years, when you reach the last budget increase, you'll have increased your income by an amount 10 times greater than the budget increases.

Even more important is the understanding that mortgage principal accelerations aren't a cost. I may have used the word *cost* for the sake of describing the increasing amount of money needed to eliminate mortgage payments. However, they actually aren't a cost. They are pure principal, including budget increases. All of it goes directly to the principal loan balance, which you are required to repay in any event. There is no escaping it. People who think they can't afford budget increases fail to realize they are simply shifting money out of the cash pocket, putting it into the equity pocket, and avoiding all the interest expense that was originally scheduled in between. The real question is whether you can afford to pay the genuine cost of interest expense. Principal accelerations have no interest expense; they're free.

Coffee Break

As a prelude to applying this information to your own mortgage, let's review what we just covered.

In addition to learning your ideal budget by referring to an amortization schedule, a conversion table, or the mortgage tables, you need to make periodic adjustments to the initial budget to offset the increasing cost of eliminating mortgage payments. This is done in two steps:

1. Adjust the initial budget by a factor relative to your interest rate. You'll find this factor in Table 13.
2. Increase your principal acceleration budget by this amount every 30 scheduled payments.

As mentioned, finding your initial budget and making timely adjustments is a rather involved process but actually is not difficult. It just seems that way. Like written instructions for changing a car tire, with all its references to the emergency brake, jack, lug nuts, and so forth, it sounds much harder than it really is. Doing it is simpler than reading about it.

To discover the right amount by which to adjust your initial budget, refer to Table 13 and find the factor relative to your interest rate. Multiply your initial budget by this factor; the product is the constant dollar amount of your adjustment.

Initial Budget $_____ × Factor _____

= $_____

The second step is to plot these adjustments every 30 scheduled payments and create an adjustment table for your own mortgage.

This system of adjustments is the key for people who start the program in midschedule. You can easily start your principal acceleration plan after having your mortgage for five years and still get right into the flow of things. Without this system, there are no benchmarks with which to get back into alignment with the program. Of course you won't save as much as if you started from the beginning, but

Table 15

Adjustment Table: Your Mortgage

Payment No.	Increase	Budget
0–30		Initial Budget
31–60		
61–90		
91–120		
121–150		
151–180		
181–210		
211–240		

that's water under the bridge. You can still save about 75 percent as much as if you started from the first payment. Don't worry about how to start in midschedule at this point; this topic will be covered in full detail in the next chapter.

 *End of Break*

The initial budget and subsequent budget adjustments that you've just learned pertain to the most powerful custom principal acceleration plan: the 5-year plan. It covers 20

years of scheduled mortgage payments in only 5 years of actual payments. Another way of looking at it is that approximately 240 scheduled payments' worth of principal have been paid in only 60 calendar months. Covering 20 years of scheduled payments in 5 actual years means that 15 years of payments have been chopped off the schedule.

Eliminating 15 years of payments is the criterion on which the initial budget and its subsequent adjustments are based. The reason I'm so keen on eliminating 15 years of payments is that a nest egg built on saving 15 years is, as I've said before, about twice as large as one built in 10 years, and it's about three times larger than one built on saving for 7.5 years. Furthermore, the savings of the 5-year plan pile up so quickly that after only 3 years of operation the plan saves more than 10 years of mortgage payments. Adopting the 5-year plan is like adopting an insurance policy. It you're forced to quit the plan early, you'll already have saved the majority of time and money.

There are situations, however, where the five-year budget is too expensive. Ironic as it may seem, there's a disadvantage to owning a mortgage with a low interest rate—the initial principal acceleration budget may be higher than you can presently afford. This is where the extended plan comes into play. It cuts your principal acceleration budget by 40 percent yet still saves about 85 percent as much time and money as the five-year plan. This may sound like a miracle, but the simple secret of the extended plan is that it is completed over a longer period of time, perhaps as long as seven or eight years. Even though it goes longer, it doesn't go beyond the point where one-third of the original balance is repaid.

We'll examine the first year that the Cliftons implement the five-year plan and then proceed to investigate how they modify the principal acceleration budget to implement the extended plan.

The Five-Year Plan

As you saw in the abbreviated example earlier in this book, the Cliftons' first normal mortgage payment is applied against payment 1. The normal mortgage payment is applied first because all interest must be brought current before any principal accelerations may be applied to principal. Paying interest on a loan that's been outstanding for the previous month is called *paying in arrears.* You may recall that your very first mortgage payment wasn't due until the following month. It wasn't that the lender was giving you a break; it's just that interest isn't due until after the loan has been outstanding for a period of time. The interest is applied first, and whatever is left over goes directly to principal. The rule that controls the application of principal and interest is also the basic rule of principal acceleration. Here it is (first introduced in Chapter 4):

Interest is computed and due only on the *actual* outstanding balance, regardless of the assumptions of the original repayment schedule.

In the Cliftons' case the interest due on $70,000 is $641.67. Since the total payment is $666.63, the remainder of $24.96 is for principal, which reduces the loan balance of $69,975.04 (see Table 6). In addition to the normal payment, the Cliftons prepay $128.29. This amount was a result of two calculations. The first was determining their initial budget of approximately $129. The second was adding the subsequent principal payments until they came closest to the $129 budget. In this case it was $128.29 (see Table 7). This principal acceleration is subtracted directly from the outstanding balance, leaving a new ending balance of $69,846.75. This is the balance at the end of payment 6. Thus the Cliftons are relieved of the obligation for payments 2–6 and thereby saved $3,204.86 of scheduled interest expense, as shown in Table 16 on the following page.

Table 16

Applying Principal Acceleration: The Cliftons

	Scheduled Interest	Scheduled Principal
Payment 2	$ 641.44	$ 25.19
3	641.21	25.42
4	640.97	25.66
5	640.74	25.89
6	640.50	26.13
	3,204.86 interest saved	128.29 principal acceleration

The First Year

Now let's take a look at how the initial budget and its adjustments are applied during the first 12 months that the Cliftons put the five-year plan into action.

The worksheet in Table 17 represents the first year of operation. "Calendar Month" is obviously the month of operation. "Regular Payment" is the scheduled payment number to which the normal payment is applied. In the first month it is 1, but in the second month it is 7 because payments 2–6 have been eliminated by the previous principal acceleration. "Budget" is the Cliftons' principal acceleration budget. You can see that it is adjusted every 30 scheduled payments. "Principal Acceleration" is the actual amount that is prepaid. "Eliminated Payments" is the number of scheduled payments that have been eliminated from the original schedule. You may say that this worksheet is the new schedule. "Interest Saved" is the amount of interest that was scheduled for the eliminated payments and that has now been saved. It will take only a few moments to learn how to read the worksheet.

As the adjustment table specifies, the average budget between payment 1 and payment 30 is $129. As you can see, in some months the Cliftons paid slightly over the budget and in some months slightly less. Likewise for the $158 and $187 budgets. Following this budget produced awesome

Table 17

Five-Year Plan Worksheet: The Cliftons

Calendar Month	Regular Payment	Budget	Principal Acceleration	Eliminated Payments	Interest Saved
1	1	$129	$ 128.29	5	$ 3,205
2	7	129	135.51	5	3,198
3	13	129	143.13	5	3,190
4	19	129	120.40	4	2,546
5	24	129	126.02	4	2,541
6	29	158	165.63	5	3,168
7	35	158	174.96	5	3,158
8	41	158	147.17	4	2,519
9	46	158	154.03	4	2,512
10	51	158	161.23	4	2,505
11	56	158	168.75	4	2,498
12	61	187	176.62	4	2,490
			$1,801.74	53	$33,530

results: more than $33,000 of interest expense has been
saved at an investment of only $1,802. This is a return on
investment of $18.61 for every $1 of principal acceleration—undoubtedly one of the best and safest investments
available to the average homeowner.

Saving so much interest is possible because of a principal acceleration budget customized to fit the changing nature of the Cliftons' particular mortgage. Starting without
it would be like starting a trip to Paris by boarding the first
plane you encounter at the airport. It might take you anywhere other than your destination.

The Extended Plan

Despite its obvious power, some people may not be able to
afford a budget of $129 per month. This is especially true
for first-time buyers or people who are buying a brand-new
home. A host of additional expenses—landscaping, drapes,
appliances, and so forth—always commands immediate

attention. Consequently some people initially need a lower principal acceleration budget. This is where the extended plan comes into the picture.

Arlene and Don are on the edge of needing the extended plan. Expressed as a percentage of their normal $666.63 mortgage payment, their principal acceleration budget is 19.43 percent. Years of experience have shown me that 20 percent is the most that the majority of people can afford, and this is on the edge of affordability. From the standpoint of dollars and cents, $129 shouldn't be overwhelming for a family making more than $35,000 a year. Furthermore, considering a possible $230,679 bank account, its reward far outshines the cost. Nonetheless, paying an extra 19.34 percent on top of the regular mortgage payment may be too big a stretch for many families. The extended plan addresses this problem and allows the Cliftons to afford a custom principal acceleration plan by virtue of reducing the initial monthly budget by 40 percent and extending the plan over a longer period of time, usually about two years longer. The net effect of accelerating a lower amount over a longer period is a budget that is 40 percent less per month yet 85 percent as effective as the five-year plan. Quite a good trade-off, wouldn't you say?

How to Use the Extended Plan

The extended plan is no more than a variation on the five-year plan. To learn the best budget for the extended plan, simply reduce the five-year budget by 40 percent. This is easily calculated by multiplying the initial budget of the five-year plan by 60 percent. Let's look at the Cliftons' situation under the extended plan. When they multiply their $129 budget by 60 percent, they arrive at a starting budget of $77.40 per month.

Five-year budget __$129__ × 60 percent = __$77.40__

The next step after learning the initial budget is to determine the adjustment amount. Fortunately, the percentage adjustment factor stays the same. In the Cliftons' case the adjustment factor is still .2275 times the initial budget amount. Therefore, their new $77.40 budget is adjusted by $17.61 every 30 scheduled payments.

Budget __$77.40__ × Factor __.2275__ = __$17.61__

(Recall that the purpose of periodic adjustments is to keep pace with the changing relationship between principal and interest as the amortization schedule proceeds from beginning to end. Otherwise the initial budget will recapture fewer and fewer payments until it's ineffective. The other approach to an initial budget and periodic adjustments plan is a single average amount, but this amount is typically too high for most people to afford. Hence, the lower starting budget and periodic adjustment approach are used to keep pace with the changing amortization schedule.)

Table 18 outlines the budget adjustments for the Cliftons' adaptation to the extended Cunningham Plan.

Table 18

Extended Plan Adjustment Table: The Cliftons

Period	Payment No.	Increase	Budget
1	0–30	$ 0	$ 77
1	31–60	17	94
2	61–90	17	111
2	91–120	17	128
3	121–150	17	145
3	151–180	17	162
4	181–210	17	179
4	211–240	17	196

Let's look at the results of the initial budget and subsequent adjustments for the extended plan (Table 19).

Table 19

Extended Plan Worksheet: The Cliftons

Calendar Month	Regular Payment	Budget	Principal Acceleration	Eliminated Payments	Interest Saved
1	1	$77	$ 76.27	3	$ 1,924
2	5	77	79.11	3	1,921
3	9	77	82.05	3	1,918
4	13	77	85.09	3	1,915
5	17	77	58.57	2	1,245
6	20	77	90.71	3	1,909
7	24	77	62.43	2	1,271
8	27	77	64.17	2	1,269
9	30	94	99.37	3	1,900
10	34	94	103.07	3	1,896
11	38	94	106.90	3	1,893
12	42	94	73.58	2	1,260
			$981.32	32	$20,321

The extended plan saves more than $20,000. And you need to prepay less than $1,000. As compared to the five-year plan, the monthly principal accelerations are more affordable. Yet the total savings are about 85 percent as good. By the time the Cliftons have finished with the extended plan, they will have saved $89,159 of scheduled interest expense and eliminated 12.8 years of mortgage payments. The economic value of 12.8 years' worth of ex-mortgage payments deposited in an installment savings account earning 8 percent per annum comes to an impressive $176,373. The extended plan is indeed an excellent alternative for people who have a relatively low interest rate and find that the budget for the 5-year plan exceeds 20 percent of the size of their normal mortgage payment. Of course it takes a couple of years longer to complete, yet its results are about 85 percent as good as the 5-year plan.

The following is a comparison of the two principal acceleration plans at the end of the program:

Five-Year Plan: The Cliftons

Months to Complete	Principal Acceleration	Eliminated Payments	Eliminated Interest
64	$15,681	180	$104,313

Extended Plan: The Cliftons

Months to Complete	Principal Acceleration	Eliminated Payments	Eliminated Interest
87	$12,835	153	$89,159

The extended plan also presents an opportunity to switch between two plans. You can start out with the lower monthly payment of the extended plan and then switch to the five-year plan as your finances improve. In addition, many people like to mix and match. They employ the five-year plan for the first three years, during which they achieve 75 percent of the results, and then switch to the lower budget of the extended plan and coast the rest of the way. Or, if you start with the five-year plan and your finances hit a lull, the extended plan provides an opportunity to switch down to the lower budget without being forced to abandon the program altogether.

There is even a Midschedule Plan for people who are picking up the program sometime after they've already been making mortgage payments. Don't worry about it now; it will be addressed later. Whether it's the midschedule plan, the five-year plan, or the extended plan, each is a better alternative than spending your entire career investing in mortgage payments and ending up house-rich and cash-poor.

The only wrinkle in learning how to use the extended plan is knowing when to quit. The five-year plan ends only after eliminating 15 years of payments. The extended plan ends whenever you reach the 2-for-1 point, even though you may not have eliminated 15 years of payments by the time you reach that point. You have to quit because it becomes too expensive thereafter. For instance, the Cliftons have examined their amortization schedule and determined that scheduled payment 248 is exactly where two-thirds of their payment goes toward interest and one-third toward principal. When implementing the extended plan, everyone must look at the schedule for his or her own mortgage because the one-third point moves according to the interest rate. On lower interest rates it appears sooner, while on higher rates it is later. The Cliftons pursued the extended plan up to payment 248 and then quit the plan.

Adjustable Rate Mortgages (ARMs Control)

The fact that the interest rate changes doesn't mean that you can't customize a plan to fit your mortgage. If there are four rate changes during the life of your program, for example, it simply means that your program will be adjusted four times as well. Yes, it's a pain to reconstruct the rest of your program every time there's a rate change, but not nearly the pain it would be to pay all that wasteful interest expense just to avoid a half hour of paperwork.

There's only one trick: don't follow the lender's statement as to your new principal and interest payment. It's incorrect! The lender's computer isn't following your progress down the repayment schedule and doesn't compute your new monthly payment based on the ending schedule number. It keeps track of only the ending balance and calendar time. If only 12 months have elapsed since the beginning of the loan, for instance, the lender will compute your new payment over 348 months. This will be true even if you've eliminated 60 scheduled payments in those 12 calendar months and your new payment should have been calculated over 300 months. Consequently, the monthly payment prescribed by the lender will be too low. It won't keep pace with the principal acceleration program. The net effect of paying this lower amount is it puts you back near the beginning of the repayment schedule.

Therefore, the first step is to determine the correct monthly P&I payment. This is easily achieved by consulting a mortgage table book or asking your friendly real estate agent, mortgage broker, or lender the correct monthly payment to amortize the outstanding balance at the time of the new rate adjustment over the actual remaining period of 300 months, for instance. This procedure is the same regardless whether the rate went up or down. Once you've found the correct amount, instead of paying the minimum asked by the lender, pay the right amount for your normal monthly payment to stay on track.

What about the initial budget and subsequent adjustments? Yes, I'm afraid those are affected as well. If the interest rate goes down, I wouldn't fuss with it, though. Your original program will exceed its original expectations. If the rate goes up, however, I recommend recalculating your starting budget and adjustments. After calculating this new plan, continue your principal acceleration program on the basis of your actual location on the repayment schedule. For example, if you've covered 60 scheduled payments, it means you're to begin your second budget adjustment. This would be the correct principal acceleration amount to achieve your original objectives.

Even though these rate adjustments are a pain in the neck, the rewards of your acceleration program are worth the extra effort. For those of you who really detest this extra arithmetic, and who also possess a computer, you can order a software diskette at a nominal cost that will do all the arithmetic for you. For that matter, you can use it to prepare any of the plans. The order forms are at the back of this book.

A Last Word and Heading On . . .

So it had come to pass that Arkad became the richest man in Babylon. When the good king, Sargon, returned to Babylon after defeating the Elamites and found his subjects wanting for the abundance of life, he called upon Arkad to reacquaint his subjects with the rules of gold. After selecting 100 volunteers, Arkad sat them in a semicircle and said:

> "Listen attentively to the knowledge that I will impart. . . . I shall teach you in simple ways how to fatten your purses. These are the seven steps leading to the temple of wealth, and no man may climb who cannot plant his feet firmly upon these steps."
>
> The first cure: "Start thy purse to fattening."
>
> The second cure: "Control thy expenditures."
>
> The third cure: "Make thy gold multiply."
>
> The fourth cure: "Guard thy treasures from loss."
>
> The fifth cure: "Make of thy dwelling a profitable investment."
>
> The sixth cure: "Insure a future income."
>
> The seventh cure: "Increase thy ability to earn."
>
> "These then are the seven cures for a lean purse, which out of the experience of a long and successful life, I do urge for all men who desire wealth.
>
> "There is more gold in Babylon, my students, than thou dreamest of. There is abundance for all.
>
> "Go thou forth and practice these truths that thou mayest prosper and grow wealthy, as is thy right.
>
> "Go thou forth and teach these truths that every honorable subject of his majesty may also share liberally in the ample wealth of our city."
>
> So Arkad did say.

6
Nuts and Bolts

I once saw an antique photograph showing farmers with huge, oversized vegetables—giant tomatoes, immense pumpkins, gargantuan squash, and other assorted produce—placed in front of their horses and wagons. Beneath the photograph was written the phrase "A pound of crop is worth a ton of theory." I've always been impressed with the remarkable common sense behind that idea. For an idea to be good, it must also be practical.

Such is the case with your customized prepayment plan—in addition to moving in harmony with the changing nature of your mortgage, it's a practical hands-on tool that provides a range of choices and opportunities. This chapter will show just how many choices you have in tailoring the program to fit your particular needs.

There isn't any new arithmetic in this chapter, just additional applications of the old material. Furthermore, each application follows one commonsense step after another until it has explored all the options in making this a thoroughly flexible prepayment plan.

Hands-On Application

The place to start the hands-on application of the Cliftons' plan is to recall the three elements in a custom prepayment plan: (1) the initial budget, (2) the adjustments to the initial budget, and (3) implementation of the adjustments every 30 scheduled payments.

We'll start this process with a review of the schedule of budget adjustments for the five-year plan of Arlene and Don Clifton. Then we'll implement the budget during the sixth and seventh months of operation. I've chosen the sixth month because it's the first time that the initial budget is adjusted. The seventh month was chosen because the budget is halfway between the actual prepayment amounts. You've already seen the first month. We'll conclude by preparing a worksheet for the first year. Along the way, we'll also look at the practical questions that people most frequently ask and answer them using applications to the Cliftons' mortgage.

Table 20

Five-Year Plan Adjustment Table: The Cliftons

Payment No.	Increase	Budget
0–30	—	$129
31–60	$29	158
61–90	29	187
91–120	29	216
121–150	29	245
151–180	29	274
181–210	29	303
211–240	29	332

Before we begin, remember that *months* means actual calendar months and *payments* means schedule numbers on the original amortization schedule.

Starting in month 6, the Cliftons' normal payment is

applied first to payment 29. Then they add another $165.63 prepayment and save another $3,168 in scheduled interest expense (see Table 21). The actual prepayment (principal acceleration) has gone up because it is at the sixth calendar month that the Cliftons have scheduled payment 30 and thus have adjusted their initial budget, as they will do every 30 scheduled payments, to keep pace with the increasing cost of eliminating mortgage payments.

Table 21

Sixth Month of Plan: The Cliftons

Payment No.	Interest	Principal	Balance
29	$ 634.40	$ 32.23	$69,175.03
30	643.10	32.53	69,142.50
31	633.81	32.82	69,109.68
32	633.51	33.12	69,076.56
33	633.20	33.43	69,043.13
34	632.90	33.73	69,009.40
	$3,810.92	$197.86	

Why is it important to keep up with the increasing cost of eliminating mortgage payments?

Without these adjustments the initial budget saves fewer and fewer payments. For instance, it had already dropped from an average of saving five to an average of saving four payments in the previous month. Adjusting the initial budget has the benefit of restoring one payment to the average number of eliminated payments. One payment may seem small, but when one payment is multiplied by the next 54 months, it becomes a large number of payments indeed. In Chapter 3 we saw that 15 years of installment deposits at $666.63 per month, earning 8 percent interest, accumulated to an investment account of $230,000. Subtract 54 months of installment deposits, and the account is reduced to $127,935. You can see that the real issue isn't whether you can afford the inconvenience of adjusting the budget but whether you can afford to lose $102,744 for want of a $29 adjustment.

Why isn't it just as good to prepay an even amount, like $150, as it is to pay exactly $165.63?

It's better to prepay the exact amount so you can keep track of your progress on the original repayment schedule. If you prepaid in increments different from those shown on the original schedule, the remainder of the schedule would be inaccurate and useless in verifying that the lender was properly applying your prepayments. Additionally, the prepayment budget has been constructed intentionally to prepay lower amounts in the beginning of the plan and higher amounts in later portions. Tipping the scale in this manner allows you to fund future budget increases out of future increases in income. If you begin to average the prepayment amounts, you may accidentally lose some of the savings. However, if you do fall off the prepayment budget, you can easily get back on by making adjustments to subsequent payments.

What about getting back on schedule if I miss a prepayment or accidentally prepay the wrong amount?

No problem. After paying your normal mortgage payment next month, simply determine your new ending loan balance, either by calling the lender or by referring to the amortization schedule. After learning your new ending balance, subtract it from the balance you would have had if you had made the payment properly and prepay the difference between the two amounts. This adjusting prepayment puts you right back in alignment with the original repayment schedule.

For example, if you omitted making the prepayment on the sixth month—and everyone does occasionally miss a prepayment—your normal mortgage payment next month would be applied to payment 30, which has an ending balance of $69,142.50. Subtracting this amount from the balance at the end of payment 34, which is $69,009.40 and where you would have been, leaves a difference of $133.10. Prepay this amount, and you're right back on schedule.

What do I do when the budget falls halfway between payments? Do I choose to eliminate the higher or lower number of payments?

This is a good question, because there will be many months when the cost of eliminating the higher number of payments pushes the total cost far above the budget yet to choose the lower number moves the cost well below the budget. Notice in Table 22 how the budget of $158 is about halfway between the total prepayments from number 36 to 39 and from 36 to 40.

Table 22

Seventh Month of Plan: The Cliftons

Payment No.	Interest	Principal	
36	$632.27	$ 34.36	
37	631.96	34.67	
38	631.74	34.99	
39	631.32	35.31	
		$139.33	Choice One
40	631.00	35.63	
		$174.96	Choice Two

The cost of eliminating payments 36–39 is $139.33, which is about $20 below the budget. If you were to eliminate a fifth month, it would push the cost up to $174.96, which is about $15 above the budget. What should you do?

First of all, there is no single correct answer. When in doubt, I suggest you prepay the higher number of payments. You can prepay the lower amount next month and vary it back and forth until the actual cost of prepayments begins to approximate the budget.

What should you do if the budget adjustment due to occur every 30 payments isn't lined up at the beginning of the month but occurs somewhere in the middle? Do you wait until next month to implement the entire adjustment?

The rule of thumb is to eliminate the highest number of payments whenever possible. Therefore, it's usually best to implement an adjustment whenever you encounter the 30th increment, even if it's located in the middle of payments scheduled to be eliminated. Implementing it in the middle of the month protects you from losing a payment every time an adjustment is made.

For example, suppose, when it came time to make the first adjustment at payment 30, the normal monthly payment was applied to payment 27 instead of 29 as it was in the previous instance. This means that payment 30 would be buried in the middle of the payments to be eliminated. Do you wait until the next month, or do you increase the budget by $29 in the middle? The rule of thumb says that you implement it in the middle, because the $29 increase will eliminate an extra payment.

Questions such as these make it clear that your custom prepayment plan is as much an art as a science. Your active participation and judgment are indispensable to the success of the program.

The Cliftons have gone on to prepay all 12 months of the first year of operation. Furthermore, they have made budget adjustments and straddled the budget on several occasions. Table 23 shows their results at the conclusion of the first year.

Table 23

First-Year Worksheet: The Cliftons

Calendar Month	Regular Payment	Budget	Principal Acceleration	Eliminated Payments	Interest Saved
1	1	$129	$ 128.29	5	$ 3,205
2	7	129	135.51	5	3,198
3	13	129	143.13	5	3,190
4	19	129	120.40	4	2,546
5	24	129	126.02	4	2,541
6	29	158	165.63	5	3,168
7	35	158	174.96	5	3,158
8	41	158	147.17	4	2,519
9	46	158	154.03	4	2,512
10	51	158	161.23	4	2,505
11	56	158	168.75	4	2,498
12	61	187	176.62	4	2,490
			$1,801.74	53	$33,530

This first-year worksheet has become the new road map to the Cliftons' mortgage. You can also look at it as a savings book. The $1,801.74 represents the cash they've switched from their cash pocket to their equity pocket, and the $33,530 is the amount of savings to date. In the future, these savings will be earning 53 months of compound interest. Even though the Cliftons can't spend the savings today, by virtue of not being required to pay the interest expense, they've accomplished the same objective—saving cash.

Don and Arlene are delighted. By saving $33,530, they've earned more than if Arlene went out to work and paid the added expenses for day care, clothing, travel, food, income taxes, and so forth. All things considered, they are saving perhaps two or three times more than Arlene's take-home pay from a full-time job. And that doesn't even consider the value of her staying close to the children as they grow up, and who can put a price on that?

Here are the results for all five years of the Cliftons' custom prepayment plan.

Table 24

Results of the Five-Year Plan: The Cliftons

Calendar Year	Average Budget Amount	Actual Prepayment	Eliminated Payments	Ending Payment Numbers	Interest Saved
1	$148	$ 1,802	53	65	$ 33,530
2	204	2,443	42	119	25,555
3	255	3,009	33	164	18,990
4	291	3,456	26	202	13,876
5	325	3,646	20	234	9,687
Totals		$14,356	174		$101,638

The thing that stands out is the far greater amount of time and money saved in the front of the mortgage. In the first three years more than $78,000 of interest and almost 11 years of mortgage payments have already been saved. Furthermore, it cost an average of little more than $2,400 per year, or a total of $7,254, to do it. Given such spectacular results, there's a natural temptation to forgo the rest of the program. Don't make this mistake!

The last two years are vital to the success of the plan, because they account for at least 46 payments. Comparing the first three years to the last two years is like comparing a boxer in the lightweight division to a heavyweight. Each is best at what he does, but they aren't comparable to one another. Underestimating the importance of the last two years is a trap, because saving time is as important as saving money. The last two years account for about 25 percent of all the time saved by the five-year plan. Forgoing them means that it will take almost four more years to pay off your mortgage. It also means you won't have those 46 months to invest in a savings account. Removing them from your nest egg means reducing it by $87,085. No one can really afford to give up $87,000.

Another thing to notice is how the budget adjustment begins to slow after the second year. That's because it takes longer to travel 30 scheduled payments in the later years than it did in the beginning of the program. This is good news, for it means budget increases won't be happening so fast that they run away from you. On the contrary, they are moving at such a steady pace that you should have plenty of time to fund these increases out of future pay increases.

The "Ending Payment Numbers" represent the scheduled payment numbers through which the custom prepayment plan has been completed. Number 234, for instance, is just short of the 20th year on the repayment schedule. That means . . . oops! Wait a minute. The Cliftons haven't reached their goal of eliminating 180 payments. They've eliminated 174 payments, which is 6 short of their goal. Does this mean that they've failed? Absolutely not; it simply means that they made judgments about implementing adjustments and about paying high or low that were slightly off the mark. There's no need to worry about missing the goal by a few payments; they can be made up easily during the following months. Perfection isn't required to be a magnificent success; mere excellence will do very well.

Arlene and Don will recover the missing six months during the first four months of the following year. It cost a little more to go beyond the one-third point, but a margin for error had already been considered in establishing it as the finish line. In fact, you can go all the way up to the point where half of your payment goes toward principal and the other half toward interest before it becomes insufferable. This 50-50 point is generally located at about payment 300. Even so, it's not recommended that you go far beyond the one-third point unless you can't help it or you have a special need to eliminate every payment you possibly can.

Ah! Now the program is complete. In little more than 5

years, the Cliftons have succeeded in covering more than 20 years of scheduled mortgage payments and saving more than $104,000 of interest expense. The icing on the cake is that they got a bonus of $4,673 on their normal mortgage payments during the period they were prepaying the mortgage. This is the reason: the loan balance at the end of payment 244 is $47,486. This means the combination of normal monthly payments and prepayments repaid a total of $22,514 in principal loan reduction ($70,000 − $47,486). This is $6,833 greater than the total of $15,681 in prepayments. Compare this $6,833 against $2,160 of credit at payment 64, which they would have received if they hadn't made any prepayments, and it's clear that their normal monthly mortgage payments received an extra $4,673 of principal loan reduction. Receiving extra credit for your normal monthly payments is the one-two punch of mortgage prepayment.

Table 25

Sixth Year of Plan

Calendar Month	Regular Payment	Budget	Principal Acceleration	Eliminated Payments	Interest Saved
61	235	$332	$ 428.15	2	$ 905.11
62	238	332	219.01	1	447.62
63	240	332	448.14	2	885.12
64	243	332	229.24	1	437.39
Subtotal			$ 1,324.54	6	$ 2,675.24
Grand Total (Rounded to Nearest Dollar)			$15,681.00	180	$104,313.00

Let's take a break!

Coffee Break

Sit back and just imagine the difference having all that extra money will make for your enjoyment of the American dream. Whether it's a golden retirement, sending the children to college, collecting antiques and taking vacations, or simply making blue-chip investments, having a nest egg of your own provides a range of choices and opportunities you wouldn't have otherwise.

As said earlier, it really cost nothing to prepay your mortgage; you've just shifted money between your cash and equity pockets. Now I can prove the same point from another angle.

By virtue of extending their mortgage repayment term from 15 to 30 years, Arlene and Don received an upgrade in borrowing power of $11,351. To buy back those 15 years of payments they prepaid a total of $15,681. This means their out-of-pocket cost was $4,331. Or was it? Actually, this $4,331 cost was offset by the $4,673 increase in principal. They actually came out ahead. Any way you look at it, it really cost nothing to prepay the mortgage.

Of course, giving up precious cash in favor of additional equity may feel like a cost. But that's the illusion that seduces people into spending a far greater number of years paying interest expense. There was never a question that the $11,351 had to be repaid. The only question was when. There once was a famous advertisement that included the phrase "You can pay me now, or you can pay me later." If you think the commercial made a good point, just remember it was referring only to the cost of a car engine.

Summarizing the implementation of the five-year plan, we can see there are three major benefits of customizing a prepayment method to fit the specifics for a particular mortgage:

1. It saves more time and money than conventional methods.
2. Normal mortgage payments get a bonus for principal.
3. It positions you on the threshold of owning a free and clear home.

This is a good time to start practicing on your own mortgage. You've already determined your initial budget and calculated your schedule of budget adjustments. Now it's time to apply these prepayment budgets to your repayment schedule and create a worksheet similar to the one in this chapter. You can start with your actual next monthly payment or at the very beginning—whatever makes you feel most comfortable. Simply apply the normal payment to the next scheduled payment and then add the subsequent schedule of principal payments until they are closest to the appropriate budget. Don't worry and fuss if you stumble the first time you try it. You also stumbled the first couple of times you tried to ride a bicycle.

 *End of Break*

The Extended Plan

As explained in Chapter 5, the extended plan is designed for people who need a lower prepayment budget than the amount indicated by the five-year plan. On 10 percent and lower-interest-rate mortgages, the initial prepayment budget exceeds our target of 20 percent the size of the normal principal and interest payment. Consequently, people with lower interest rates may find the extended plan more to their liking.

The extended plan costs 40 percent less than the five-year plan, and it takes a couple of extra years to complete. It's precisely because the plan is in operation for a longer time that it still saves approximately 85 percent as much time and money as the five-year plan. Lowering your budget by 40 percent yet losing only 15 percent of the reward is why the extended plan is such a viable alternative.

Other than taking longer to complete, the extended plan is implemented just as the five-year plan is: the procedures are the same, the paperwork is identical, the worksheets operate in the same manner, the same rules apply, and the same fine-tuning techniques are employed.

Table 26 is the Cliftons' budget for the extended plan.

Table 26

Extended Plan Adjustment Table: The Cliftons

Payment No.	Increase	Budget
0–30	—	$ 77
31–60	$17	94
61–90	17	111
91–120	17	128
121–150	17	145
151–180	17	162
181–210	17	179
211–240	17	196
241–300	17	213

Let's look at the results of the extended plan. Since it works just as the five-year plan, there's no need to go through a month-by-month review. Instead, we'll go directly to the worksheet for the first year and then skip ahead to the conclusion of the plan.

Table 27

Extended Plan Worksheet: The Cliftons

Calendar Month	Regular Payment	Budget	Principal Acceleration	Eliminated Payments	Interest Saved
1	1	$77	$ 76.27	3	$ 1,924
2	5	77	79.11	3	1,921
3	9	77	82.05	3	1,918
4	13	77	85.09	3	1,915
5	17	77	58.57	2	1,245
6	20	77	90.71	3	1,909
7	24	77	62.43	2	1,271
8	27	77	64.17	2	1,269
9	30	94	99.37	3	1,900
10	34	94	103.07	3	1,896
11	38	94	106.90	3	1,893
12	42	94	73.58	2	1,260
			$981.32	32	$20,321

As you can see from Table 27, the extended plan operates just as the five-year plan. However, the extended plan doesn't encounter payment 30 until the ninth month, when the Cliftons make a $17 adjustment in the budget. The first time they encounter the decision about whether to pay above or below the budget, however, occurs in the fifth month. Other than the timing of these decisions and adjustments, everything remains the same.

Of course the amount of time and money eliminated from the schedule is less, but so is the amount of investment. The rate of return on the savings, however, is still very comparable to $20.73 of interest saved for every $1 of principal prepayment.

Since we are jumping so far ahead on the schedule, can we ever skip a normal monthly mortgage payment?

The answer is absolutely not! Remember, one of the four rules of a mortgage is that you must pay the minimum monthly mortgage payment for however long the mortgage is in existence. This rule precludes ever missing a payment.

Even the business firms that convert your fixed monthly mortgage into a biweekly mortgage adhere to this rule. Although you pay into an escrow account biweekly, they pay your mortgage out of the account monthly. It's by virtue of making 26 biweekly payments, instead of 24 semi-monthly payments, that there's excess money to make a prepayment at the end of the year. This explains why there are no savings during the first year. The excess isn't accumulated until the end of the first year, so your savings don't show up until the second year. In fact this method moves so slowly that it usually takes about five years just to make up the service fee charged to establish the escrow account.

Table 28

Results of the Extended Plan: The Cliftons

Calendar Year	Average Budget Amount	Actual Prepayment	Eliminated Payments	Ending Payment Numbers	Interest Saved
1	$ 48	$ 982	32	44	$20,351
2	104	1,258	28	84	17,407
3	125	1,592	25	121	15,074
4	148	1,842	21	154	12,158
5	163	1,977	17	183	9,356
6	179	2,259	15	210	7,741
7	196	2,276	12	234	5,724
7+	196	651	3	240	1,349
Totals		$12,837	153		$89,160

In the case of the Cliftons' 11 percent mortgage the extended plan stopped at payment 240. This is where one-third of the original balance on an 11 percent mortgage has been repaid and precisely where two-thirds of the payment goes toward interest expense and the other one-third toward principal loan reduction. Payment 240 is the same one-third point for all 11 percent mortgages, regardless of how large or small the original balance.

How do I switch between the extended and five-year plans?

This is a great question, because many people like to follow the more powerful five-year plan for the first three years and then switch to the extended plan when the monthly cost starts to get higher. When they switch to the extended plan, their budget actually goes down. From there on they coast the rest of the way.

There are two primary ways of switching between plans. The first method is to find a point on the worksheet where both plans have the same ending or outstanding loan balance. Now that you've found that common point, next month simply prepay the budget for the plan you wish to switch to. For example, the two plans coincide at payment 66. Instead of prepaying the amount indicated by the five-year plan, you would pay the amount indicated by the extended plan. Presto! You've just switched between the two plans.

In the event that there isn't a matching balance at the time you wish to switch plans, the other method is to make an adjusting prepayment. Similar to how you got back on track when you missed an entire payment in the earlier section, this method calls for you to make an adjusting payment between the two plans. For instance, if the Cliftons were following the extended plan and just finished with payment 33 and wanted to switch to the five-year plan, they would check to see whether there was a match. In this case there isn't. The closest one is at payment 35. This means they could pay the next normal payment, thus erasing payment 34, and wait until next month to begin the five-year plan. Or they could prepay payments 35–40 and start next month on payment 41.

Starting the Plan in Midschedule

Many people will start their custom prepayment plan after they've already paid their mortgage for several years. The system of budget adjustments is exactly what you need to pick up the program in midstride.

1. Refer back to the coffee breaks in the previous chapter and bring forward the initial budget and subsequent budget adjustments on your personal mortgage.
2. Prepare a worksheet for the plan of your choice, starting from the very first payment. The purpose of starting from the beginning is to learn the proper budget for your current location on the repayment schedule.
3. Start prepaying your mortgage with the budget relative to your position on the worksheet. For example, if Arlene and Don didn't begin the program until after they had their mortgage for 3 years, or 36 months, and their plan of choice was the extended plan, they would pick up the program between the 10th and 11th months of the worksheet. If you refer back to Table 27, you will see that payment 36 falls between these two months. The decision at this point would be whether to wait until regular payment 38 or prepay between the months as discussed previously and begin the program immediately. Either way, starting the program three years into the life of their mortgage presents no problem for the Cliftons. Without this handy scheme of budget adjustments, it would be very difficult to customize a prepayment plan once they had already started paying their mortgage.

What if I want to make up for some of the lost payments? How do I recapture payments I would have eliminated had I started from the very first payment?

Once again the answer lies in the worksheet. In the case of the Cliftons, if they picked up the program in the 11th month, they would finish out the year by eliminating 5 payments (see Table 27). These 5 payments are 27 payments short of the total 32 payments outlined on the worksheet. The Cliftons are keen on recapturing these 27 payments because they know they can make a substantial difference in the size of their eventual nest egg. Therefore, aiming to recapture 27 payments over the remaining life of the program becomes the Cliftons' objective.

They can go about it in two ways: first, they can make a lump sum payment and recapture most of them all at once. Second, they can average the amount of the lump sum payment over the remaining life of the program and recapture them bit by bit. This latter method is the mid-schedule plan.

The Lump Sum Method

The easiest way to calculate the lump sum payment is to total all the principal prepayments up to the point where you pick up the plan. For instance, if the Cliftons pick up the plan on the 11th month at payment 38, the total prepayments up to that point are about $800. Consequently, a lump sum payment of $800 will recapture many of the 27 lost payments.

It doesn't recapture all of them, however, because $800 now buys fewer payments than it did at the outset of the program. If you wish to get the equivalent of all 27 payments, add up the principal scheduled for the next 27 payments on the repayment schedule and pay that exact amount. For instance, the total amount of principal scheduled for payments 39–66 on the repayment schedule is $1,121. Paying $1,121 instead of $800 will recapture all 27 payments.

Making a lump sum payment adds another wrinkle to the administration of your program. Now that you've recaptured the 27 payments in a lump sum and jumped ahead to payment 66, you will pick up the rest of the program starting with payment 67, not payment 42. Remember, it's the actual outstanding balance that controls all interest payments. Pay the principal through payment 66, and there's no place to start other than payment 67.

Unfortunately, most homeowners don't have an extra $1,121 to recapture lost payments with a lump sum prepayment. The alternative to coming up with all the money at once is to pay a little of it at a time. This is where the midschedule plan can help.

The Midschedule Plan

This is the way the midschedule plan works. In addition to eliminating the number of payments specified on the worksheet, simply eliminate an extra payment or so every month until you've recaptured all the lost payments. For example, after the Cliftons determined that they wanted to make up 27 lost payments, they learned they still had about 78 months remaining in the program. A typical extended plan has about 90 months, and a 5-year plan has about 60 months. In the Cliftons' case the extended plan had a total of 88 months; since they had passed the 10th month, the remaining number was 78 months. This means they have to make up an average of one payment every 3 months to recapture the lost payments before the end of the program. As a practical matter, the earlier they recapture them the cheaper it will be, as the average cost begins to really climb in the latter sections of the mortgage.

The proof for the number of remaining months in the Cliftons' plan is in the following formula, which you can use with your own mortgage.

Remaining Time Calculation

Last Payment before program	37
Payments that should have been eliminated	<27>
Number of months allocated	10
Number of months in entire program	<88>
Number of months remaining	78

Of course, the short formula is simply to subtract the 10 payments to date from the total number of months and you have the same answer.

Other than the addition of extra payments to the normal schedule of budget adjustments, the midschedule plan is managed exactly as the extended and five-year plans. Naturally, you'll have to prepare a new worksheet to account for the extra payments, but that shouldn't be a problem since the schedule of budget adjustments remains unchanged and everything is implemented as before.

Let's take our last break.

Coffee Break

If you started the program late, now is the time to decide whether you want to make up for lost payments. If the answer is yes, you can either make a lump sum payment or prepare a midschedule plan.

The first step in calculating the lump sum payment is to complete this chart:

Number of payments to recover   _____

Current location (payment no.)   _____

Projected location (payment no.)   _____

Principal between two points $_____

A lump sum payment of this amount will recover the number of payments lost by starting late.

If a lump sum payment is too expensive, the midschedule plan is your best alternative. The first step in this process is to determine the number of calendar months remaining in the equity program by plugging your data into the following chart. Remember, the 5-year plan has 60 months, and the extended plan has approximately 90 months.

Increment   _____

Months that should have been eliminated   _____

Difference = number of calendar months   _____

Number of calendar months in program   _____

Number of remaining months in program   _____

 *End of Break*

A Last Word and Heading On . . .

It's important to have a practical custom prepayment plan that also provides a range of flexibility. You can choose the most powerful five-year plan, the more affordable extended plan, or mix and match between the two. You can miss prepayments, make mistakes, start late, and still be assured of saving the most time and money available. Customizing the plan to fit your personal mortgage provides all the tools needed to really take charge of your biggest and best investment. The custom prepayment plan helps you get it all.

This chapter concludes Part II, the how-to part of the book, and sets the stage for Part III, which deals with related prepayment issues. The first of these chapters deal with the myths that attempt to make a virtue of debt. These are what I call "yeah, but . . ." arguments. As you might guess, that's the title of the next chapter.

PART III
MYTHS
AND TIPS

7
Yeah, But . . .

The story "The Three Little Pigs," is a delightful fairy tale. As I said in Chapter 2, I like fairy tales because they convey an essential truth about life. They put you in the middle of the action and make it clear that your personal qualities make all the difference in the outcome. Fairy tales are fundamentally different from myths. Myths, in this context, take away your power and give it to forces outside your control—the economy, government, or capricious gods, for instance. It is they who have the power, not you. Ultimately myths leave your security and peace of mind to hope and good luck. Hence the moral of the Three Little Pigs is not a myth.

You may have heard one or more of the arguments against mortgage prepayment. You also may have noticed that a good part of their argument concerns the wisdom and virtue of debt. Looking a bit deeper, you'll discover these arguments have a striking resemblance to myth. In addition to taking away your power, they suggest that you rely on hope and good luck. They encourage you to hope that the reward of debt will eventually be greater than the real cost of it. Don't bet your life on it. Being hopeful that something will eventually turn up is the kind of myth that leaves 70 percent of Americans house-rich and cash-poor at retirement.

Furthermore, the arguments in favor of debt and against mortgage prepayment sound good until you look beneath the surface. Then you discover that most of the people who believe these arguments also subscribe to the "micturate upwind" effect.

The 13 Seductive Myths of Debt

The enticing thing about most of the arguments in favor of debt is that they may have been true at one time. Consequently, they seem to make good sense. However, as soon as you look beneath the surface, you can detect a fatal flaw in each of the arguments.

The following is a list of the 13 most common objections to the wisdom of principal prepayment.

1. "I need the tax deduction. I can't give up my interest payments."
2. "I can't afford to prepay my mortgage."
3. "Yeah, but I plan on moving within five years. I'll never pay off the mortgage on this house."
4. "Wouldn't I earn just as much by putting the prepayment money in a bank account instead?"
5. "Yeah, but it's better to borrow dear dollars today and repay them with cheapened inflation dollars 25 years from now."
6. "I believe inflation will return and appreciation will bail me out."
7. "Money should always be moving; otherwise it isn't working."
8. "Yeah, but aren't normal mortgage payments already a form of forced savings?"
9. "Perhaps I should refinance and get a lower interest rate on a new 30-year mortgage."
10. "The payoff isn't for 15 years, and it's not worth waiting."

11. "Isn't 'nothing down' the new game in real estate?"
12. "Yeah, but what about the prepayment penalty?"
13. "Yeah, but I just don't see how real estate prices can go down. There is only so much land to go around.

1. "I need the tax deduction. I can't give up my interest payments."

You keep virtually all of your tax deductions at the same time as you eliminate interest expense. This may sound like a paradox, but remember that prepayments are in *addition* to the normal monthly mortgage payments. These normal mortgage payments are loaded with interest expense, all of which is still tax-deductible. Your actual tax deduction doesn't really begin to fall until the last 5 years of the mortgage. Since you are going to reach this point in any event, you might as well get there 15 years early and save all the mortgage payments in between.

The fact that you keep virtually all your tax deductions during the same period that you are making prepayments can be seen in the first year the Cliftons implemented the prepayment plan. They saved more than $33,000 in scheduled interest expense. Yet, remember, every month they were still making a $666.63 mortgage payment, the bulk of which was interest. Since more of their normal payment starts going toward principal, their tax deduction is about $50.00 less than if they didn't make prepayments. If the Cliftons are in the 28 percent net tax bracket, this lower tax deduction will mean an actual increase in taxes of only $14. Eliminating more than $33,000 of scheduled interest expense while paying $14 extra in tax is a trade-off that I'd be only too happy to make.

It appears that one reason tax deductions are considered untouchable is that many people confuse tax deductions with real money. They often believe the two are the same thing, because they fail to understand the practical difference between a tax deduction and a tax *credit*. A tax credit is a dollar-for-dollar reduction in the amount of taxes you owe the government. A tax deduction, on the other hand, is a reduction in the amount of income that is *subject* to taxation. A tax deduction, such as interest expense, effectively excuses certain income from taxation and saves the taxpayer an amount of money proportional to his or her tax rate. For example, if you are in the 28 percent tax bracket, you would normally be taxed $.28 for each $1 of income. However, for each $1 that is spent on interest expense your tax bill is reduced by $.28, which is good news. The bad news is the homeowner loses $.72 in the transaction.

If there is no alternative but to make interest payments, then taking all possible deductions is the smart thing to do. However, it's not a good idea to spend a dollar just to save $.28 in taxes. This is a good way to go broke saving money. Fortunately, a prepayment plan offers the best of both worlds. It eliminates the worst of the interest expense and lets the homeowner keep the best of tax deductions.

Viewed in a larger picture, not all tax deductions are for spending money. There are also tax deductions for saving money, such as IRAs and Keogh plans. Once you've paid off the mortgage 15 years early, you can replace the loss of tax deductions for interest expense with a higher-quality tax deduction for *saving* money. An IRA or a Keogh is a higher-quality tax deduction because it defers 100 cents on the dollar from taxation. This is almost four times larger than tax deductions for interest expense. The cash value of a tax deduction for spending money is limited to your tax bracket. If you are in the 28 percent tax bracket, for instance, the tax refund is limited to $.28 for each dollar of interest expense. So, the benefit of a $1.00 tax deduction for saving money is almost four times greater than the $.28 refund for spending money. Exchanging saving dollars for spending dollars is a great way to build a bigger nest egg.

Furthermore, the interest income on these IRAs and Keoghs is also tax-deferred. This means that your savings account will grow faster because interest is compounded on interest without the interference of taxes. Moreover, your tax rate after you are retired and begin withdrawing these funds may be less than before retirement.

You come out a tax winner from at least three angles:

1. You save $1.00 rather than only $.28.
2. Interest earnings are greater on $1.00 than on $.28. Also, the earnings are tax-deferred, which means they will compound and grow more quickly.
3. The tax rate on withdrawing the savings may be substantially less than prior to retirement.

Moreover, the trend in taxation is moving away from deductions for wastefully spending money and toward offering tax incentives to increase productivity and save money. Although they still have a long way to go, this is the essence of the Tax Reform Act of 1986. In short, the government has decided to stop subsidizing speculation in debt by eliminating the tax deduction for most interest expense. Eliminating incentives to spend money wastefully makes perfect sense; after all, tax deductions are designed to cushion the blow of interest expense, not eliminate the pain altogether. It's not an accident, either, that the United States has the lowest savings rate in the industrial world, while Japan has the highest. The United States gives tax deductions for spending money, and Japan offers tax deductions for saving money. It's clear that increased saving is in the best interest of the family, the financial system, and the country as a whole.

Interest on mortgages has been largely spared at this point, but even this sacred deduction has been mentioned more than once as a possible candidate for adjustment. There is a message in this: don't base your financial security on current tax policy and the promises of government. Government policies move according to the winds of political expediency.

2. "I can't afford to prepay my mortgage."

At the risk of sounding inconsiderate, you can't afford *not* to prepay your principal ahead of schedule.

Let's look at the question from a fresh perspective. What must you pay? You must repay the principal that you originally borrowed. What needn't you pay? All of the interest scheduled on your mortgage. If you were Don or Arlene Clifton, which could you better afford to pay, the $33,000 of scheduled interest expense as well as the $1,800 of principal or the $1,800 of principal ahead of schedule? The answer is obvious: it's cheaper to pay the $1,800 ahead of schedule than it is to pay the $33,000 of interest expense as well. There's no other choice.

3. "Yeah, but I plan on moving within five years. I'll never pay off the mortgage on this house."

In fact the benefits of a prepayment plan move with you to the new house. You can use the additional equity to buy a bigger house or take a shorter-term mortgage on a house of approximately the same value as the old one. Once you own a dollar of equity, you never lose it simply because you switched houses.

The argument that prepayment is wasted on the old house confuses your financial net worth and your mortgage. The mortgage indeed expires when you sell your current house. Fortunately, however, your financial net worth and the additional equity in the old mortgage move with you to the new house. You can use them in one of at least two ways. First, you can take a shorter-term mortgage on the new house. For instance, suppose you implemented the custom plan over a 5-year period and are on the 20th scheduled year with only 10 years remaining on a 30-year mortgage by the time you decide to move. Instead of taking a 30-year mortgage on the new house, you take a new 10-

year mortgage and effectively transfer the benefits of the plan from one house to the other.

A case study will illustrate the point. The Clifton family implemented the custom plan and eliminated 15 years of its original 30-year amortization schedule. Those 15 years of eliminated payments combine with 5 years of normal payments to move the Cliftons to year 20 on the repayment schedule. If the Cliftons were to buy a new house of the same or lower cost, they could take out a new 10-year amortized loan, keep the same monthly payment, and effectively transfer the 15 years of eliminated payments to the new house.

In terms of dollars and cents, this means that the combination of prepayments and normal payments repaid about $22,500 of an original $70,000 balance. The unpaid balance stands at about $47,500. This is the outstanding balance at payment 244 on the amortization schedule. If the Cliftons buy a new house, contributing their hard-dollar equity and any appreciation equity as their down payment, they may need to finance no more than $47,486. It would be silly to take a new 30-year mortgage and return to "Go." The better idea is to leave the monthly payment unchanged and take a 10-year mortgage on the new house. The Cliftons could afford the 10-year mortgage because the borrowing power of $666.63 per month at an 11 percent interest rate is approximately $47,486, as we saw in the Initial Gain section. Thus their financial net worth moves with them to the new house and mortgage. The value of prepayment is never lost because you simply moved houses.

Of course, it's human nature and the nature of penny-wise and dollar-foolish ideas to ignore the opportunity of a 10-year mortgage in favor of the lower monthly expenses of a long-term mortgage. But it's a trap to take a new 30-year mortgage every time you move. Suddenly people wake up at age 49 with a new 30-year mortgage and realize that they'll be 79 years old before they're scheduled to pay off the mortgage. Considering that only 5 percent of the entire population earns more than $25,000 per year after retirement, the chances that you will have enough money to keep making mortgage payments and also have enough for the other necessities are pretty slim.

However, if you haven't reached middle age, there's another way to use former prepayments. You can use the additional equity to buy a bigger or more expensive house. Use it as a down payment and leverage a larger balance on a 30-year mortgage. Considering that you can usually borrow $4 for every down payment dollar, prepayments and additional equity in the old mortgage can help you buy the dream house you could not afford otherwise.

In summary, you never lose the benefits of mortgage prepayment simply because you change houses. You can move as many times as you wish and afford to take a slightly shorter mortgage each time. Who knows? Perhaps you will have the luxury of taking a five-year mortgage on your last house.

4. "Wouldn't I earn just as much by putting the prepayment money in a bank account instead?"

There are several reasons why this argument doesn't hold up. First, prepayment saves far more money. Second, the chances that the money in the savings account won't be touched for 30 years fall somewhere between slim and none. The very fact that liquidity is considered an advantage of a savings account is evidence enough that that money will never survive the duration. Third, prepayment is forced savings. Finally, in times of emergency, you can always borrow against the equity in the house. It's not an either/or situation; you can have both.

Even if it were to remain untouched for 30 years, exclusive investment in a savings account accrues to about half of the amount accrued by prepayments. This is true despite the fact that interest on the alternative earnings is being earned and compounded for a longer period of time. It doesn't approach the savings of prepayments, because prepayments start by saving about $19 for every $1 investment, while the alternative earnings start with perhaps $.08 on the dollar. Thus the earnings rate never catches up to the savings rate of the prepayments.

The critical points of comparison are the 15th and 30th years. At the 15th year the alternative earnings approach has money in the bank, but the homeowner still owes the majority of the original loan balance. By the 30th year the custom plan is far richer than the alternative earnings plan.

5. "Yeah, but it's better to borrow dear dollars today and repay them with cheapened inflation dollars 25 years from now."

The logic of this argument is that the buying power of money in 25 years will be only a fraction of what it is today, so it is smart to stay in debt for 30 years to take advantage of the cheaper money. The catchphrase is "borrow dear and repay cheap."

This is a compelling statement until you look at how it works in practice. If you remember the true cost charts in Chapter 3, you will recall that interest expense in the first 5 years is $19 for each $1 of equity. In contrast, the cost during years 26–30 is only $.30 for each $1 of equity ownership. This argument would have you pay the $19 expense today just for the privilege of paying $.30 of expense with cheaper dollars in 25 years. The fatal flaw of the "repay cheap" axiom is obvious: the buying power of the money used to pay today's $19 interest expense is much greater than the buying power of the money that will be used to pay the $.30 in interest expense 25 years from now. Paying exorbitant interest cost with today's most valuable dollar is a great way to go broke. The cheap-dollar argument is a classic example of being tricked into watching one hand while the real magic is being performed with the other.

If this equation were turned around, and it were possible to pay the $19 interest with inflation-riddled dollars 25 years from now, it would be a great strategy. However, that's not the case. It appears that this "repay cheap" argument is an attempt to sugar-coat the assumption that you are resigned to 30 years of mortgage payments. The bitter pill of debt is sweetened by saying the cost gets cheaper the longer you own the mortgage, so it's OK to take 30 years to pay off the mortgage. Don't believe it!

6. "I believe inflation will return and appreciation will bail me out."

The threat of inflation is never far away. The national debt and annual budget deficits, combined with a questionable economy, make inflation a tempting quick fix to a problem with few solutions. However, the return of high inflation probably won't be accompanied by high appreciation. Instead homeowners will probably win the booby prize and experience high inflation and relatively low appreciation.

Today inflation and appreciation operate differently than they did during the era of profitable debt. Then inflation pulled appreciation up; now inflation will tend to hold appreciation down. The difference is interest rates. In the earlier era interest rates were held artificially *lower* than the inflation rate, and appreciation was pushed up. Now interest rates are *higher* than the inflation rate, which will hold appreciation down. The Federal Reserve Board changed its policy and decided to allow interest rates to float according to the market forces of supply and demand. So long as they hold to this traditional approach, high inflation will continue to mean higher interest rates, which in turn means lower appreciation.

High inflation without corresponding high appreciation would be the worst of all worlds: everybody loses. Imagine a housing market with 16 percent mortgage rates (created by a 10 percent inflation rate) and accompanied by a 5 percent appreciation rate. There would be few buyers, and resale values would stagnate. Not only would sellers be stuck, but every homeowner would suffer a 5 percent annual loss in the capital value of his or her house. This is the spread between the 10 percent inflation rate and a 5 percent appreciation rate. The return of runaway inflation would be a financial nightmare for homeowners.

Of course, all things are possible. It is always possible that the government will get into such trouble that national economic policy will change and politicians will attempt a quick fix of cheap money. Germany tried the same thing in the 1920s, and it only worsened the situation. Not only did inflation ruin the economy, but it also created a backlash that spawned the Nazi party.

Even if we were extraordinarily lucky, and high appreciation attended high inflation, you must remember that it's not appreciation that has you chained to your job but your debts. There is no escaping them; you can either pay them now or pay them later. Unfortunately, paying them later may cost your entire career.

7. "Money should always be moving; otherwise it isn't working."

Actually, saving money is just as important as earning it. The $1 that's invested to save $19 of interest expense isn't idle but working harder than ever. This is a 1,900 percent return on investment, which is guaranteed and 100 percent risk-free. Moreover, it liberates 15 years of mortgage payments, which eventually provide a large enough savings account to make all your dreams come true. Even Ben Franklin would have been impressed by your prudence and foresight.

The idea that money is idle if it's invested as equity in the home is a leftover from the days of profitable debt. At that time everyone concentrated on paper money and not cash. The popular yardstick was profit margin. The larger the debt, the larger the potential profit margin. The profit margin was at its largest when hard-dollar equity was at its smallest. This strategy is known as *leverage*. Less equity in one investment also meant more money available to invest in other appreciating assets, and profits were multiplied. This latter strategy was commonly known as *parlaying*. Parlaying and leverage are still viable concepts for investment property, provided the asset is keeping pace with inflation and someone else is paying the interest expense through rent payments. However, your home is not a commercial investment, and it is not a tenant who is paying the mortgage but you.

A shortsighted objection is that a large amount of equity will make a house more difficult to sell. The fear that if there is a lot of equity there can be only a small assumable loan, and therefore the house will be more difficult to sell, is unfounded. For example, a home selling for $100,000 with a $50,000 assumable loan may not be more difficult to sell because the prospective buyer is required to have a $50,000 down payment.

In fact a large amount of equity may help sell a house. The more equity you have in a house, the more favorable terms you can offer a prospective buyer in the way of secondary financing. The interest rate and terms in the form of a second mortgage can be adjusted to fit the needs of the buyer. For example, a buyer who needs $30,000 of additional financing can borrow a portion of it from you. If you own $50,000 of equity, the buyer can borrow $30,000 from you at the prevailing rate and make a $20,000 down payment. You have accomplished the primary task of selling your house and also own a $30,000 mortgage note.

After all, the buyer's first concern is actually the purchase price. The amount of your equity doesn't affect the purchase price. Furthermore, assumable loans are fast becoming the Model Ts of mortgage lending. The "due on sale" clause in mortgage documents is being strictly enforced by most lenders, and therefore the assumability of a mortgage is often a moot point. Consequently, continuing to make mortgage payments that are largely eaten by interest expense, simply to satisfy a need that might not exist in the first place, isn't good common sense.

In contrast, building equity offers a greater number of choices: you can take a second mortgage, lower the sales price, rent the property, or enjoy a variety of opportunities. Given the choice between making it easier for yourself and making it easier for the real estate agent, take care of yourself first.

8. "Yeah, but aren't normal mortgage payments already a form of forced savings?"

Receiving credit of only $1 for every $20 paid into an account can hardly be called forced savings, let alone an investment. That's what happens to normal mortgage payments during the first five years of an 11 percent mortgage. Actually, it's prepayments and not mortgage payments that are genuine forced savings. For every dollar you invest in prepayments, you save $19 of interest expense. This, indeed, is forced savings.

The basic misunderstanding between mortgage payments and forced savings starts when people fail to distinguish between appreciation and cash. Granted, equity does indeed accumulate, but that doesn't make it a savings account, for equity isn't cash. You can't spend equity at the grocery store. The difference in spendability is only the first of many differences between a genuine savings account and equity. There are many more differences:

S stands for savings account.
H stands for house.

S—A savings account permits withdrawals as well as deposits.
H—Equity in a house cannot be withdrawn at will.

S—A savings account generates cash in the form of interest earnings.
H—A house constantly consumes cash in the form of maintenance, taxes, insurance, repairs, special assessments, and so forth.

S—The dollar value of a savings account isn't dependent on local conditions but is the same across the country.
H—The value of real estate fluctuates with the local housing market.

S—A savings account is liquid and can be converted into other higher-earning assets at the owner's will.
H—Equity in the house is not liquid; it is frozen in place.

S—You can borrow against a savings account.
H—Once you retire, it's extremely difficult to borrow against the equity in the house because a retired homeowner doesn't have a salary with which to qualify for a new mortgage.

Debt is paid with hard cash, while appreciation is merely paper profits. Ending up with paper profits but without cash is a trap. This distinction is so subtle that most people get trapped into believing that there is no difference between their home and a savings account. Sales agents imply that mortgage payments that are largely interest payments are just forced savings.

Another very important difference between a home and a savings account isn't financial but emotional. Money in a savings account can be withdrawn and spent with little remorse, while the only way to spend the equity in a home after retirement is to give up one of life's most cherished possessions. This is an emotional loss from which many people never recover. Yet conventional wisdom would have you believe that the home is your best savings account and making mortgage payments for 30 or more years is the same thing as investing in a savings account. This is a fabrication.

Mortgage payments are actually forced spending, not forced savings. Only prepayments are forced savings. First, they push you into the latter stages of the amortization schedule, where the amount of principal in each payment is substantial. Second, they eventually eliminate 15 years of mortgage payments. These payments, in the case of the Cliftons, result in a $230,000 savings account. Thus prepayments are the only forced savings that you cannot afford to do without.

9. *"Perhaps I should refinance and get a lower interest rate on a new 30-year mortgage."*

It doesn't need to be a choice between refinancing and prepayment. You can have them both. If the new interest rate is sufficiently low, you can reduce your monthly payment and also shorten the term of the new mortgage. If it isn't low enough to accomplish both, then perhaps you should consider shortening the term ahead of reducing the monthly payment. You shouldn't go back to a 30-year term unless there's no other choice. The reason is simple—it's the length of the mortgage and not the interest rate that adds the greatest cost to a mortgage.

An 8.5 percent *30-year* mortgage, for instance, will cost far more than a 12 percent *15-year* mortgage. If you refinance a mortgage to lower the monthly payment but start over again on a new 30-year payoff schedule, you've fallen into a seductive trap. The cost of a mortgage more than doubles for each new 5-year extension of the repayment period. This doubling, or compounding, effect, is so powerful that the effective cost of an 11 percent mortgage grows from a low of 30 percent to a high of 1,915 percent. This 1,915 percent is the effective cost of acquiring equity ownership during the first 5 years of mortgage payments on an 11 percent 30-year mortgage. The solution to the high cost problem is to first cut the length of the repayment term, and then attempt to reduce the monthly payment. (See Chapter 9, "Tips," to learn how to get both a shorter term and lower mortgage payments.)

Many people also believe they shouldn't prepay their "cheap" 8 percent mortgage, especially when the prevailing interest rate is higher than their existing mortgage. This is also a seductive argument because most people don't realize that their true cost isn't $.08 on the dollar but a cost that's far higher. During the first five years of an 8 percent mortgage the cost actually is $7.93 of interest expense for each dollar of loan principal loan reduction. The focus should be on the cost to acquire equity and not the cost to support debt. Therefore, looking at the 8 percent end of a mortgage is like looking at a donkey from the wrong end, the dangerous end.

10. "The payoff isn't for 15 years, and it's not worth waiting."

Actually the savings are immediate. As soon as you prepay the principal, you're immediately relieved of the obligation to pay the scheduled interest expense. Since saving money is the same thing as earning it, the payoff is immediate.

At the heart of this objection is the belief that if it's not in your hand it's not real. It's true that you can't spend it yet, but that doesn't mean the savings aren't real. Whether it must be in your hand before it is real was addressed thousands of years ago by Chinese sages when they observed that it is the hollow space in a bowl that gives it purpose. Likewise the empty space in a wall is the essence of a window, and the vacant space between the spokes of a wheel is what provides its strength. These attributes may be invisible to the naked eye, but they're as real as granite.

It seems that the misconception starts with the belief that the mortgage payments saved via prepayment are effectively subtracted from the end of the mortgage. Therefore the benefit isn't received until you reach the end of the mortgage. They see the mortgage being cut from 360 months to 354 months, and so on until it is paid off. Actually, you start at payment 1, jump ahead to payment 7 for instance, and march toward payment 360. This is a very important distinction, for the amount of interest you save by eliminating payments at the beginning of the mortgage is far greater than the interest that can be saved at the end. In addition to saving more money, eliminating them from the front of the mortgage means the savings are immediate.

Another subtle yet immediate benefit is the additional amount of principal being credited to your normal monthly payments. Once the Cliftons finished their custom plan they were in the *last* 10 years of the repayment schedule. The average principal reduction (equity buildup) is $295 per month. A person who didn't prepay is still in the *first* 10 years of payments where the average principal reduction is only $57. Thus the prepayment person is earning $238 more per month than the nonprepayment person. The situation is even more dramatic during the following 5 years. The person who accelerated his or her equity payments receives $510 of loan payoff, while the other person gets only $99, a difference of $411 per month. Yet both people pay the same $666.63 per month. Admittedly, you have to wait until the mortgage is paid off before you can spend or invest the cash, but the actual savings are immediate.

11. "Isn't 'nothing down' the new game in real estate?"

Nothing is "for nothing." If you pursue schemes such as using various government programs to buy distressed properties, be careful that you aren't the distressed seller next year. These situations are distressed because there are problems associated with the property. Experts in the field of distressed properties indeed make money at their profession. However, amateurs often lose their proverbial shirts. They're usually dependent on things outside their control, such as appreciation, to come out as winners.

12. "Yeah, but what about the prepayment penalty?"

The prepayment clause usually doesn't say what most people think it does. It still exists in some loans, but fewer than you might imagine. Very few mortgages since 1980 even have prepayment clauses. Furthermore, prepayment penalties are prohibited by many states and in most government-insured loans. Check your loan documents or consult an attorney to learn whether your mortgage contains a prepayment penalty.

Do not despair if your loan does in fact have a prepayment penalty clause. This dog's bark is worse than its bite. The reason is simple—the penalty is hundreds of times less than the amount of interest saved by aggressive prepayment.

For example, the typical penalty clause is invoked on annual payments that exceed 20 percent of the balance. The penalty would apply only to that portion exceeding the 20 percent limitation. The stiffest penalty calls for 90 days' interest on the principal over the 20 percent benchmark. For example, the penalty on a $5,000 payment over the 20 percent maximum on an 11 percent $70,000 mortgage would be approximately $137.50 ($5,000 × 11 percent for an annual cost of $550 × ¼ year = $137.50).

This is the cost side of the equation. What is the benefit side? The 20 percent limitation on a $70,000 loan equals $14,000. If the Cliftons were to exceed their limitation by $5,000, it would mean the total prepayment in one year was approximately $19,000. A $19,000 prepayment during the first year of their mortgage would jump them approximately 217 payments (18 years) and save about $126,000 of interest expense.

Is there any question that a $137 prepayment penalty is worth saving $126,000 of interest expense and immediately eliminating 18 years from the repayment schedule? Add the opportunity to earn interest income for 18 years to the initial savings, and the total benefit amounts to an astounding $320,000. Prepayment penalties are indeed toothless dragons.

Actually the prepayment penalty is not a direct reflection of the banker's attitude toward accelerated payments. Prepayment penalties are really directed against mass refinancing when the prevailing interest rate is lower than earlier rates. It discourages people from playing a game of musical mortgages, changing to a new mortgage every time the rate changes.

Although bankers may wring their hands at the thought of more paperwork, they realize the rewards are worth it. They win from at least four perspectives. First, foreclosures are reduced. The quality of the loan becomes higher when more equity is invested in the house; few people desert their homes when only 9 or 10 years are left on the mortgage. Second, the banker's liquidity is improved by virtue of receiving an extra 15 percent of the original loan over a 5-year-period, yet the accelerated payments are not so large as to disturb their assets-to-liabilities ratio. Third, they keep loans on the books for a longer time. Fewer people are enticed to refinance their mortgages to lower the rate a point or two when they've already saved more than 60 percent of all the interest scheduled on their current mortgage. Accordingly, the lender may receive higher income for a longer period of time. Finally, the bank can use the proceeds to fund another mortgage to a new customer and earn additional points and fees. Everyone wins: you, the bank, and the next customer.

13. "Yeah, but I just don't see how real estate prices can go down. There is only so much land to go around."

Now it's my turn to say, "Yeah, but. . . ." The value of land—the price that someone is willing to pay for it—is determined more in the mind of the buyer than by any appraisal. If people perceive that land is both desirable and scarce, they will bid the price higher and higher. However, if people firmly believe that land is neither scarce nor desirable, the price will fall like a rock. The marketplace votes with its dollars.

We needn't go any further than the Depression of the 1930s to witness the fall of real estate prices, land in particular. The term *dirt-poor* wasn't a compliment. Millions of people owned a lot of land but didn't have a nickel to buy a cup of coffee. It was many years before these people could be persuaded to own real estate again. And even with 2 and 3 percent mortgages, they still got out of debt as soon as possible. In their minds real estate debt was inherently a liability, not an asset. They weren't the first generation to learn that the relationship between price and scarcity is a fragile one.

The most famous story about this fragile relationship and the effect of psychology on the value of any given commodity is the Dutch Tulip Bulb Mania of 1635. Tulips first came to Holland from Turkey in the mid-1500s, growing steadily more popular until it was deemed that every person of culture should own some. Unfortunately, they were still relatively rare. So scarce were they that it was not uncommon for a single root to fetch 2,500 florins. The following list shows what a person could buy with 2,500 florins in 1635:

	Florins
Two lasts of wheat	448
Four lasts of rye	558
Four fat oxen	480
Eight fat swine	240
Twelve fat sheep	120
Two hogshead of wine	70
Four tuns of beer	32
Two tuns of butter	192
One thousand pounds of cheese	120
A complete bed	100
A suit of clothes	80
A silver drinking cup	60
	2,500

Although I haven't the slightest idea what a "last" of wheat or a "tun" of beer is, I still think it is quite an expensive tulip root, don't you? By the year 1635 it was common for many people to spend 100,000 florins for the purchase of just 40 roots. Considering the proven market for such a scarce commodity, it's understandable that the roots were eventually sold on the stock exchange of Amsterdam, Rotterdam, and elsewhere.

It wasn't long before everyone got into the act. Whether it was a wealthy merchant or a simple chimney sweep, everyone was converting assets into cash and buying flowers as quickly as possible. After all, the rich of the world were coming to Holland and buying as many tulips as they could get their hands on. Everyone imagined the passion for tulips would last forever. But it didn't.

Unfortunately, as reported in *Extraordinary Popular Delusions and the Madness of Crowds*, first published in 1841 and still in print, people with a longer view of things began to realize that someone had to lose in the end. As soon as they pulled out of the market, confidence broke and the market for tulips collapsed. Many a fortune was ruined in the tulip mania, and it was decades before the economy of Holland got back on its feet.

Indeed, history proves that the value of a commodity is no higher or lower than a buyer is willing to pay for it. The tulip mania was no exception; history is riddled with other manias. A commodity has little inherent value of its own. Real estate goes up and down as does every other commodity. Furthermore, there's actually no scarcity of land; there's more in the United States than we can possibly use.

Any number of factors can set economic momentum moving in a negative direction. For example, an industry on which the entire community depends could have a disastrous year. There could be a recession in the economy. Political upheaval or a bankrupt government could start a negative trend. It could even begin with the affairs of a taipan in Hong Kong. If you think that it is a far-fetched idea, just remember that the First World War started with the assassination of an obscure duke in Serbia. Just as people were at the mercy of history in 1914, so are you subject to international and national events that could start the price of real estate moving in the wrong direction.

The following is but one possible chain of events resulting from momentum moving in the opposite direction. Before long, it turns into a downswing in home prices.

1. Consumer demand drops as empty pocketbooks, the disappearance of profitable debt, and a new premium on cash take the allure away from debt.
2. The number of homes on the market increases as fewer homes are absorbed by lower consumer demand.
3. Prices are reduced to lure scarce buyers. As price falls, there is no incentive to buy today because the price may be lower tomorrow.

4. Desperate homeowners put homes on the rental market in an attempt to cover cash requirements, thereby forcing supply of rentals to grow.

5. More homes for rent means lower rental rates. Speculators get washed out of the market as their cash flow from rentals falls below the mortgage and upkeep payments.

6. Renting becomes an attractive alternative to owning. More renters means fewer buyers.

7. Sales among existing homes stagnate as new homes capture a larger share of the market because builders have more bargaining room than the typical homeowner.

8. Lenders begin to restrict their lending policies when they see the value of their collateral falling, the level of foreclosures increasing, and the number of personal bankruptcies at an all-time high. These restrictions disqualify more buyers, thus lowering demand even further.

9. New investment money is drawn away from residential housing to liquid assets, such as the stock market or risk-free T-bills, which earn a genuine return above the inflation rate.

10. Lower demand eventually means lower interest rates, which provides an even greater incentive for buyers to wait and see.

11. The cycle becomes self-perpetuating, as was the case when the market was moving on the upswing.

A downward spiral in prices is surprisingly difficult to see in the beginning, for it is often hidden by an antiquated reporting system that tends to show only the rosy side of the picture. For example, the National Association of Realtors reported at their national convention in November 1987 that Denver and Houston were suffering the worst resale markets in the country. Yet it also reported that average prices rose 4 percent in Denver. How can prices be both rising and falling at the same time? The answer lies in the fact that these reports represent only one type of house and only if that house actually sold. Nonconforming houses and all houses that didn't sell are completely ignored. Even if the number of unsold houses is 10 times greater than the number of sold houses or if people cannot sell their houses at any price, that information goes completely unreported.

Fortunately, you needn't be wiped out if prices begin to fall. Once you reduce your level of borrowing and start paying less interest expense, you'll be in a better position to weather the storm. At worst you'll pay less interest on a house that is worth less. At best you'll be able to use your savings and buy a bigger and better house that now also costs less.

A Last Word and Heading On . . .

It's a myth to believe there's a greater reward for spending your entire career making mortgage payments. Unless you're extraordinarily lucky, you can't afford to pay the exorbitant interest expense during the first half of a 30-year mortgage and still have enough left over for retirement, education for the children, vacations, and so forth.

Rather than staying in perpetual debt and relying on good luck for your well-being, a better alternative is to prepay a selective portion of your mortgage. Your mortgage is one of the few things over which you have absolute control, and it is also your biggest opportunity to reduce your level of borrowing and save cash. Finally, it operates in perfect accord with Abundance Rule 2 and reduces your vulnerability during times of stress and uncertainty. You can't lose.

In the next chapter you'll learn how simple it is to put your custom prepayment plan into action. Most of the steps rely on nothing more than common sense and good information.

8
Housekeeping

I n addition to prepaying the ideal amount of principal, the only other secret to a successful prepayment program is to work in harmony with your lender and keep adequate records.

In the course of this chapter we'll explore the administrative details and paperwork that should be coordinated with your lender. They include

- notification requirements,
- prepayment clauses,
- requirements for separate prepayment checks,
- verification of outstanding balance,
- avoiding escrow accounts,
- date of credit for principal prepayment,
- planning worksheets,
- miscellaneous.

Lenders Are People First

Before considering the details, I think you should realize that the lender is your friend, not your enemy. Due to a few bad apples, however, most bankers and mortgage lenders have a worse reputation than they deserve. This unfortunate reputation leads most homeowners to believe the lender will automatically be against principal prepayment. Many times I have heard, "If I'm going to save money, the lender must be against it." Nothing could be further from the truth. Bankers actually enjoy their greatest profit when their customers are prosperous, not when they are suffering. Naturally lending institutions deserve to make an honest profit. Profit is merely nature's way of saying they will be in business next year. Accordingly, it's simply a case of enlightened self-interest for lenders to support programs that enhance the financial health of both their customers and themselves.

There are at least four ways the lending institution profits when you prepay your mortgage.

1. They will reloan the money to another customer and have two loans instead of just one.
2. They earn points and fees on the new loan, which has been partially funded by your prepayment.
3. They have the opportunity to retain the money and increase their liquidity and safety.
4. Most important, the likelihood of foreclosure on a mortgage that's been prepaid is reduced to virtually zero. In these days, foreclosures are a lender's greatest headache. Prepayments greatly increase the quality of the loan and all but eliminate the risk of foreclosure.

Finally, and as a bonus, the lender may actually be able to keep a loan on the books for a longer period of time when it's been prepaid than if it hasn't been prepaid. The reason is simple—there's less incentive for the homeowner to refinance. The homeowner already may have saved over 60 percent of the interest expense. It's too much trouble, and the fees and points probably aren't worth trying to save another 10 percent or so. Consequently the lender keeps 85 percent of the original loan, which may be at a higher rate than the one to which everyone else is refinancing. Considering these five benefits, it's clear that prepayment rewards the lender as much as it benefits you.

Above all, the reason lenders will support your prepayment plan is that they are people first. They have the same cares and concerns as you and I. They have children to raise, bills to pay, and mortgage payments to make. A program that works for you would also work on their own home.

Communication

A smooth plan starts with good communication. Good communication means nothing more than you and the lender understanding each other's intent. Once both of you understand and agree how the program will proceed, techniques are a secondary consideration. The mutual intent of each party becomes more important than the process. If a glitch occurs, it will be easy to rectify, because both parties are operating with the same scorecard. It's when the two parties have a different understanding and expectations that glitches are difficult to remedy.

The first step is for you to do your homework and read your mortgage documents. I know they're as dry as a bone, but these documents often lay out the ground rules for what may be called "prepayment" or "principal curtailment." Each lender is different, so these requirements may vary greatly. Many lenders have no requirements at all, while others have detailed, and sometimes confusing, requirements. If the mortgage documents are too confusing, hire an adviser for an hour or two. The cost of his or her advice isn't an expense but an investment. For instance, many lenders have deleted the prepayment clause altogether. Their intent is to eliminate all prepayment considerations, yet by not mentioning prepayment they may have inadvertently created doubts about whether it is permitted. Happily, these ambiguities are simple to clarify, and advisers that give you peace of mind are worth every penny.

Prepayment Clauses

Prepayment penalty clauses are a case in point. As discussed in the preceding chapter, those that do still exist are intended merely to protect lenders against wholesale refinancing of loans every time the prevailing interest rate goes down a point or two. Even when penalty clauses do exist, as the example in Chapter 7 showed, the savings incurred by prepaying in excess of the 20 percent limitation are worth the penalty.

Yes, it's important to know all the stipulations about the prepayment penalty, but no, it's not something to fear.

Notification

The most common notification requirement is 30 days' written notice. This gives the loan servicing department ample opportunity to prepare for your specific program. Many mortgage documents are silent on this point, but it is nevertheless wise to give the servicing personnel as much preparation time as possible. It is in your best interest to learn their operating procedures so your prepayments are submitted in a manner consistent with these procedures.

Lockboxes

Virtually all mortgage lenders use a "lockbox" procedure. The term *lockbox* comes from earlier days when there was actually a locked box at the bank in which people deposited their money. Nowadays the term still applies to a certain procedure for collecting money, but the actual box no longer exists. Lockboxes are used to help lenders get immediate credit for your payment at a commercial bank by depositing your check a day or two before doing the bookkeeping on your account. These one or two days are especially valuable if the lender is located in a different state from the customer. For example, WestAmerica Mortgage Company, which is based in Colorado, has more than 23,000 customers spread over seven states. Instead of waiting several days for the mail to reach them, they use a post office box in the local community, collect from it several times a day, and deposit the payments in a local commercial bank. By saving one or two days of uncollected funds on 23,000 customers, the lender saves huge amounts of money. Consequently, chances are great that your lender uses a lockbox procedure.

Ordinarily, you wouldn't be concerned with the operating procedures of the lender. However, lockboxes are a different matter. They affect your prepayment plan in that your prepayments will probably be administered by hand, and not by a computer, and in that one check with both the normal monthly payment and the prepayment will be better than two separate checks.

The reason your prepayments will be processed by hand is that the commercial bank that collects the money in the lockbox also performs an initial bookkeeping entry. The bank has a computer listing of all the payments scheduled for that month, and if the actual payment is more or less than the scheduled dollar amount, the bank removes it from the system and sends it to the mortgage lender for special handling. Therefore, most prepayments will be kicked out of the computer system and credited to your account by a real live person in the loan servicing department.

This is a great opportunity. It means that your prepayment plan will receive the personal touch. Once you and the person in the loan processing department understand one another, chances are great that your monthly payment will be handled without a hitch. It also means that you have a real person to talk to if ever the need arises. It all comes back to the idea that lenders are people first; treat them as such, and you're already halfway to a smoothly running program.

One Check or Two?

The use of a lockbox also implies that one all-inclusive check is better than two checks. Some people think writing two checks is better because the homeowner will have a separate check for a record of the prepayment. This is true in theory but not in practice. One check is the best way to ensure that your prepayments will be applied as intended.

One check that combines the normal monthly payment and the prepayment avoids problems that can occur when half of the bookkeeping is done at the lockbox end of the process and the other half is done by the loan processing personnel. One check bypasses the lockbox procedure and puts all the bookkeeping in the servicing department. Any number of things can go wrong when the functions are split up. For example, the checks could become separated during lockbox processing. Anything can happen if the prepayment is separated from the normal monthly payment. One of the checks could get lost or delayed. One of the checks could be put in the drawer by a new clerk and forgotten. Another possibility is that each check could be applied to the opposite purpose. The prepayment could be applied against the normal monthly payment, for instance. This is not a disaster in itself, but it would create a real paperwork problem that might take hours upon many frustrating hours to work out. This is especially true if the two payments are applied at different times. Given that the lender works the same hours as the customer, it may be weeks before a letter is sent and you have an opportunity to resolve the problem.

All of these unnecessary headaches could be avoided by tendering one all-inclusive check. Of course, if your lender demands two checks, you may have no choice but to proceed as requested. A demand for two separate checks is just another good reason to communicate with the loan servicing personnel and satisfy yourself that they have considered these issues and can properly handle two checks. If so, by all means proceed as requested.

Escrow Accounts

Escrow accounts are financial holding pens. It's where money is parked while waiting for something else to happen. Your objective is to stay out of an escrow account.

First of all, your money isn't receiving credit, not even interest income, while it's in an escrow account. People usually end up in an escrow account because the servicing personnel don't know what to do with the prepayment. Either there were no instructions or the customer never contacted the lender to learn the appropriate procedures or there was a glitch between the lockbox and the lender's servicing department. Aside from poor communications, the next biggest culprit for landing you in an escrow account is paying with two checks. For instance, if one of the two checks is misplaced and a clerk doesn't know what to do with your second check, your payment will probably be deposited in an escrow account. Once that happens, one of the two checks will languish and won't be applied until a later time. There are also other snafus that could land you in an escrow account, and some bad apples have been known to play games with the escrow account, but it's usually the mishandling of two separate checks that gets most people into trouble.

Date of Credit

Another major reason for avoiding an escrow account is the common practice of crediting your principal prepayment on the actual day it is received. Unlike the normal monthly payment that has a grace period during which the payment is credited back to the first of the month, principal prepayment is usually credited on the day actually received.

This doesn't present much of a bother. If you normally pay your mortgage payment on the fifth of the month, it means that your initial prepayment will be credited on the fifth of the month, and your record of the outstanding balance will reflect a tiny difference from the lender's records. However, if you continue paying on the fifth of the month, each of your subsequent prepayments will be at 30-day intervals, and your plan will be relatively on track.

Landing in an escrow account knocks you off track, however. Since your prepayment doesn't receive credit until it comes out of escrow, which may be a month or more if the lender has to write a letter asking for instructions, the amount of interest you think you've saved hasn't been saved at all. This is another good reason for submitting only one check. If there's not a second check, it can't get separated into an escrow account and lose the interest you intended to save. Even if it's their mistake, the bank probably won't backdate your prepayment to the day it collected it but to the day it resolved the mystery.

Although more and more lenders are beginning to backdate normal and prepayments alike, precisely when your prepayment will be credited is another topic for discussion with your lender. Will personnel backdate the credit if they mishandle the prepayment? If there is a substantial delay between the date they cash the check and the day they do their bookkeeping, should the credit for your prepayment also be delayed? None of these are difficult questions for the lender and you to resolve, yet if they're left unaddressed they can cause more trouble than necessary. It's a repeat of the old adage about an ounce of prevention being worth a pound of cure.

Records

Records and paperwork are a pain in the neck, but only when there aren't any. Records are never a pain when they can answer questions. And have no doubt, questions will arise. It's not a question of *if* but of *when.* Memory will not suffice. Regardless of how fresh and important the information appears today, your memory won't be a tenth as reliable next year. Furthermore, even a saint would go insane trying to rummage through five years of haphazard prepayment records. As a matter of protecting your own sanity, you need to keep a separate file on your prepayment plan.

This file may be organized in any way you see fit; however, it is best to check first with the lender to learn what information would be helpful in researching a difference between its records and yours. The common approach is to organize it in chronological order, by month. It should contain evidence of payment, such as canceled checks or copies thereof, all acknowledgments from the lender as to the ending balances, all correspondence with the lender (including notes on telephone conversations), the amortization schedule, and planning worksheets that you may have used in setting forth your prepayment program, and so forth. These records are usually sufficient to resolve any misunderstanding or problem that may occur. They also serve an additional purpose; they establish your credibility with the lender.

The most basic record of all is the trusty amortization schedule. Simply draw a line through each scheduled payment as it is paid off. What a great pleasure you'll experience as you strike all those payments off the schedule! Before you know it, you'll be years ahead of schedule. Of course, the normal mortgage payment pays off one month, and the prepayment knocks off a whole group of them at a time. At the end of the line, note the date, check number, and amount of each payment.

For example, in the first month of the Clifton's mortgage, the first line corresponding to payment 1 is crossed out by virtue of the normal monthly payment. The Cliftons also included a prepayment of $128.29, so the next five lines—which represent the next five scheduled payments and reduce the principal by $128.29—are also lined out. This eliminates payments 2–6. The normal mortgage payment eliminates scheduled payment 7 in the subsequent month, and another prepayment of $135.51 would eliminate the subsequent five scheduled payments, and so forth.

Amortization Schedule as a Record: The Cliftons

Scheduled Payment No.	Interest	Principal	$70,000 Balance
1	$641.67	$24.96	$69,975.04
2	641.44	25.19	69,949.85
3	641.21	25.42	69,924.43
4	640.97	25.66	69,898.77
5	640.74	25.89	69,872.88
6	640.50	26.13	69,846.75
7	640.26	26.37	69,820.38
8	640.02	26.61	69,793.77
9	639.78	26.85	69,766.92

Keeping track of your progress on the amortization schedule is as simple as ABC. You can see exactly how far you've come and can use the outstanding balance to check your records against those of the lender.

Verification of the Outstanding Balance

One good use of records is to check your outstanding balance against the lender's record of your balance. It is an excellent idea to do this several times a year if not monthly. If there's a discrepancy, you can resolve it immediately. If an undue amount of time elapses between cashing your check and crediting your principal, you will discover it. If your prepayments are landing in an escrow account, you'll know it. In short, checking your outstanding balance is an excellent way to learn whether your program is running as smoothly as possible.

One way to verify the outstanding balance is the amount on the monthly statement. Lenders who do send monthly statements simplify the verification process because the outstanding balance listed on the statement should reflect the last prepayments. However, rather than monthly statements, a great many banks provide yearly coupon books. Unlike monthly statements that show the outstanding balance, the coupon book shows only the scheduled balance. As soon as you make your first prepayment, these balances are no longer accurate. It is only at the end of the year that lenders who use coupon books send their customers a statement showing the outstanding balance. Therefore, unless you call the loan servicing department each month to inquire about the balance, you may not realize there is an error until the end of the year. Correcting a problem after it has festered for a year is far more difficult than correcting it after only a month or two.

As a side note, some of these statements and coupons have a space for listing the amount of your principal prepayment. Use it whenever possible. Clearly listing the amount and purpose should further reduce the possibility of someone's misapplying your money.

In summary, filing your records in such a manner that you can easily research a question will save you countless hours of frustration. In addition to avoiding problems, good records help create opportunities, because they are the starting point for good planning.

Planning

The amortization schedule is a great way to verify the outstanding balance and also actually see the amount of time and money that you're saving. However, it tells you only where you've been, not where you're headed. For this purpose you'll need to modify the amortization schedule and create a planning worksheet.

There are several good reasons for preparing a planning worksheet. First of all, knowing where you're headed gives you the opportunity to change your mind or plans if you don't like the destination. For instance, you can increase or decrease the prepayment budget. Second, it also helps you budget ahead. Finally, your discussion with the loan servicing personnel will achieve its best results if there is a specific prepayment plan to discuss. You and the lending institution can compare the projected outstanding balance at the end of each of the five years in your custom plan and determine whether your figures agree with theirs. If they match, you will know that both parties are operating under the same set of assumptions, and, except for occasional errors, the plan should proceed as smoothly as silk. If they don't match, it is an unparalleled opportunity to resolve the difference before implementing the prepayment program.

The planning worksheet is essentially a modification of the old amortization schedule. The worksheet eliminates some of the old information and adds new information. The worksheet has three new columns. The first new column records the prepayment amount. The second new column shows the number of scheduled payments eliminated by the prepayments. The third new column shows the amount of avoided interest expense.

The following planning worksheet represents the consolidation of the Cliftons' amortization schedule and prepayment program for the initial two months. Of course, you are free to label the columns any way you wish. The nomenclature isn't important; being sufficiently accurate so you can foresee the future and plan ahead is very valuable.

Payment No.	Principal	Prepayment	Number Eliminated	Schedule No.	Interest Saved	Outstanding Balance
1	$24.96	$128.29	5	2-6	$3,204	$69,846.75
9	26.37	135.51	5	8-12	3,197	69,684.87
13	etc.					

The merit of a planning worksheet is starting to emerge. Fifteen lines of scheduled payments have been consolidated into two lines. Previously scheduled principal has been totaled into the "Prepayment" column. The months that have been eliminated are shown in the "Number Eliminated" column. Previously scheduled interest expense is now shown in the "Interest Saved" column. At the very least, prepare a worksheet at the beginning of each year, and you'll know your destination at the end of the year before you even start.

These three new columns are only the minimum. You can add as many others as seem useful. Some people like to add columns to distinguish the results for a single month from accumulated results. For example:

Month	Number Eliminated	Accumulated Eliminations	Dollar Value	Accumulated Value
1	5	5	$3,204	$3,204
2	5	10	3,197	6,401

In the first month the monthly and accumulated columns are the same. In the second month, however, the accumulated columns report the sum of the progress to date. For example, the monthly "Dollar Value" column reports a savings of $3,197, and the "Accumulated Value" column totals $6,401.

As mentioned earlier, one purpose of a planning worksheet is to learn whether your plan delivers the desired results before it is implemented. You can experiment with the best strategy to achieve these goals if you ask "what if" questions, vary the assumptions (such as budgeted prepayments), and determine the impact on the overall results. Remember, a small increase in the prepayments has a dramatic effect. The custom plan calls for periodically increasing the prepayments to eliminate an average of one additional scheduled payment per month. Taken by itself, this one month seems insignificant, but taken over 48 months, it amounts to a very substantial four years of mortgage payments. Four years of avoided mortgage payments means four years of additional savings, which is worth a great deal of money.

Another question might be "What if the IRS refund (or

another lump sum) is added to the program? How far ahead would I jump; how much extra money would be saved? Would it help me make up for lost time if I started the program late?" The planning worksheet can answer other similar questions, such as the wisdom of taking a short-term loan to eliminate the most expensive sections of the repayment schedule. The possibilities are endless, but the answers will remain hidden unless you operate from a planning worksheet.

A critical question that the worksheet answers is whether you will complete the program prior to the point where one-third of the original balance has been repaid. If not, you have the opportunity to take corrective action by increasing the budgeted amount or adding lump sum payments. The objective of the custom plan is to complete the program before you reach the one-third point. As soon as one-third of the original balance has been repaid, the average cost to eliminate additional payments begins to build rapidly, and soon it is too expensive to continue. That's why we call this point *the wall.*

You can still save a lot of money going beyond the wall. For a while at least, you'll save $2 of interest expense for every $1 of principal prepayment. A 200 percent savings rate is still a pretty good return on investment.

Targeting the prepayment plan to be completed at the one-third point also provides a margin of error. In the event that you don't save enough time and money by the time you reach the one-third point, you have room to continue prepayments before it becomes absolutely too expensive. It becomes absolutely too expensive to prepay your mortgage as soon as one-half, or 50 percent, of the original balance has been repaid. This is the actual point of diminishing returns, the point where the savings are actually less than the cost of prepayment. Furthermore, the speed that costs are increasing and savings are falling is astonishing. It is impossible to keep up with the mounting costs. The plan must be abandoned at this point.

Fortunately, there are only about five years left on your mortgage by the time you hit this point. Paying nothing more than normal mortgage payments will retire the other 50 percent of the original balance in approximately five years because the average equity buildup after the one-half point is 76 percent of the normal payment on an 11 percent mortgage. This is when mortgage payments are really getting their money's worth.

These are only some of the benefits of creating prepayment worksheets and planning ahead. In addition to helping you budget your finances and learn about the amount of time and money you can save, they give you a frame of reference for discussions with the servicing department of your lending institution.

Miscellaneous

Don't be surprised if you become the local expert in principal prepayment. Even in the mortgage banking industry, and especially at the clerical level, few people know the ins and outs of prepayment as clearly as you do now. In fact, don't be surprised if your first inquiry to the lender is met with a bewildering reply. Don G. Campbell, a syndicated columnist writing for the *Los Angeles Times*, the *Denver Post*, and a number of other newspapers, has recommended easy mortgage prepayment ideas to his readers for quite some time, and he reports that several of his readers have received some very strange responses from lenders. Do not despair; simply seek a higher-level manager until you find someone who will help you.

A Last Word and Heading On . . .

It's only natural to feel a little nervous at the prospect of discussing these issues with your lending institution. After all, they held all the power when you last applied for a mortgage. This time, however, the situation is different.

This time you probably know more about mortgage prepayment than they do. Furthermore, you are helping them as much as they are helping you. Again, they receive at least five rewards when you prepay your mortgage. Finally, don't forget that they're people first. The commonsense details outlined in this chapter will also help make their job easier.

In addition to these housekeeping details, the next chapter offers some practical tips for fitting the prepayment program into the rest of your daily life: hidden sources of money for prepayments, a unique way to shop for a house, refinancing opportunities, and so forth. These ideas are just starting points; your imagination is bound to improve them many times over. In fact, I'd love to hear about your creativity and success in prepaying your mortgage. Please write to me, in care of the publisher, about your prepayment story.

9
Tips

This chapter is devoted to practical ideas that will help you implement your prepayment plan. And it is your prepayment plan, not mine. Arlene and Don Clifton have already named their program "The Clifton Prepayment Plan." Thousands of others have done likewise. I hope you follow their example and add your name to the title of the plan.

The tips in this chapter cover a wide range of topics. They include hidden sources of prepayment money, creative definancing, shopping for a home, new mortgage programs, refinancing options, pitfalls, the safest places for your savings, and so forth. The ideas expressed in these tips aren't intended to be the final word, but rather spark plugs that will help you start thinking about new and creative ways to make your program as successful as possible.

Prior to discussing these tips, however, I think it's important to remember that a positive attitude is more powerful in creating positive results than mere techniques alone. I realize that this is just a fancy way of saying "Where there's a will, there's a way." Yet it is so true that it bears repeating. Undoubtedly you will run into obstacles to continuing your prepayment plan. Your attitude and determination at those times will be the key ingredients in removing such obstacles.

In a similar fashion, some people give more power to their limiting beliefs than to their opportunities. These beliefs include such things as "I don't have enough money, I'm not smart enough, rich people aren't nice people so I don't want to have a lot of money, they'll never let me do it," and so forth. These beliefs are a trap that leave people impotent before they start. Since you've made the effort to reach the last chapter, however, I doubt these limiting beliefs have control over your life. Nonetheless, everyone periodically experiences some of these doubts. When they do come up, it's important to recognize that there is a difference between limiting beliefs and practical considerations.

Naturally certain practical considerations must be taken into account. That's the purpose of this chapter: practical answers to practical considerations. These answers take the perspective that considerations aren't fences that prevent you from reaching your destination but simply hurdles to be jumped as you continue your journey.

Money

The first consideration on everyone's mind is money. "Where am I going to find the extra money for the prepayment plan?" Actually there are a number of hidden opportunities. There are cottage industries, part-time jobs, delayed purchases, windfalls, and so forth. For instance, Arlene Clifton earned all the money that her family needed by operating a part-time telephone answering service that earned about $25 to $30 a week. This is but one example of a cottage industry that is ideally suited for a homeowner. Picture the homemaker with two children who stays home all day. Taking care of the children may be one of society's and the family's most important jobs, but neither society nor the family gives the job the understanding, salary, and status it deserves. Yet Arlene's $30 a week is just as responsible for creating the eventual $230,000 bank account as is her husband's regular paycheck. In the first year alone, the Cliftons eliminated 53 months of mortgage payments worth more than $33,000 in scheduled interest expense. As mentioned earlier, this is the equivalent of a $46,000 salary taxed at a 28 percent effective tax rate. How many jobs allow a person to stay home, take care of the children, and still earn $46,000?

Cottage Industries

There are more cottage industries than you might imagine. A wonderful book written by Shebar and Schoder, *How to Make Money at Home*, lists 73 such industries and tells the reader how to get involved in these areas. Here are 20 examples of cottage industries:

Day care	Furniture refinishing	Answering service
Typing	Telephone sales	Gardening
Messenger service	Shopping service	Market research
Dog walking	Crafts	Baking
Cooking classes	Childbirth preparation	Music lessons
Sewing	Sewing classes	House-sitting
Housecleaning	Hairstyling	

Many of these jobs seem unglamorous and pay only minimum wage. Consequently, many people who stay home think they are hardly worth the effort. Plus, there is the additional expense and problems of day care for the children, chores to put aside for another day, and so forth. Yet from the perspective of the prepayment plan, a part-time job paying a few dollars an hour for seven or eight hours a week can translate into an effective income of $46,000 a year. Quite a respectable way to spend a few hours a day!

Part-time jobs are not just for the homemaker. Everybody can pitch in. Your son can contribute a share of his earnings from the paper route, and your teenage daughter can likewise donate a portion of her earnings from the bookstore. This is a great opportunity for everyone to be a valuable and contributing member of the family.

Budgeting

In addition to cottage industries and part-time jobs, the person or people responsible for the monthly budget can often dig up hidden money. Impossible as it may seem at first blush, there might be some extra money hidden in the budget. For example, perhaps the car is going to be paid off soon. Instead of buying a new car, you can convert the old installments over to prepayments. After all, the monthly prepayment budget is often less than the cost of buying a car. Have you researched the cost of a new car lately? Even an "economy" car probably costs more than your entire prepayment program. Delay purchasing a new car for a couple of years, and you've got it made. Someone once told me that new car purchases account for more money than people spend on their houses. I've never added it up, but it might be a revealing insight to see if that statement is true.

In a similar vein, are you considering buying more furniture or another refrigerator? If so, step back and think about last year's big purchase. The pleasure fades pretty quickly, doesn't it? The point is this: there is probably more money in the budget than you imagine, but to find it your attitude makes all the difference. After all, you may be looking for no more than *2½ percent* of your total monthly budget. Traditionally, to qualify for a mortgage about 25 percent of income should be applied to the mortgage payment. If the beginning budget of the extended plan calls for a 10 percent increase in the mortgage payment, then the prepayment equals about 2.5 percent of total income (.10 × .25 = .025). Operating in proportion to your monthly income is one of the hidden gems of the prepayment plan.

Windfalls

Another tip is to look to the future for extra money—pay increases, for instance. How about allocating 25 percent of future pay raises to the plan? Don't forget; you qualified for the original loan based on the traditional ratio of approximately 25 percent. Now that your income is increasing, it's only appropriate that your mortgage payment should also increase.

This idea is good theory as well as good practice. You were probably forced into a 30-year mortgage because your previous income prevented you from qualifying for a shorter-term mortgage. Now that the 30-year mortgage has enabled you to obtain ownership, its primary job is ended. However, you are left with the huge expense of having added the final 15 years of mortgage payments. You can solve this problem and eliminate the extra 15 years of payments by allocating pay increases to maintaining the ratio of 25 percent of your income to mortgage debt retirement. It's a good idea whose time has come again.

There are other sources of money that we tend to forget about. The most obvious, which many people tend to forget, is IRS refunds. Congress enacted the tax deduction on mortgage interest to help the average home buyer reduce the effective cost of buying a home. What better way to act out the spirit of the law than to use your tax refund to eliminate 15 years of mortgage payments and use that money to build a nest egg for retirement?

Another source of money for lump sum payments is windfalls. In ancient times it was forbidden to pick fruit from the trees of noblemen, but it was permissible to eat whatever fruit fell off the tree of its own accord or was blown off by the force of the wind. Whenever the commoners found fruit on the ground, it was a sign of good luck. Thus the term *windfall.* There are many windfalls—bonuses from work, prizes, bequests, gifts, lottery winnings, overtime pay, inheritances, and so on. All of them can be powerful financial allies.

Creative Definancing

One of the more creative ways to find a lump sum for prepayments—though it may sound like heresy—is to borrow it from a commercial bank. This is not for everybody; it's recommended only for those who have a fair amount of experience in borrowing money for investment purposes. If the Cliftons borrowed $5,400 from a bank and paid it against the principal loan balance, they would immediately eliminate the first 10 years of mortgage payments and save $75,000 of scheduled interest expense. Assuming the loan is paid over 3 years at a 10.5 percent interest rate, their monthly payment on the $5,400 loan would be about $175. This means that they would repay a total of $6,300, which amounts to an extra $900 in interest expense. Thus the Cliftons would end up about $74,000 ahead of the game by borrowing the prepayment money. Actually the $900 cost is even mitigated by additional credit for principal on the normal mortgage payments. Instead of the payments starting with a credit of $24 for principal at payment 1, they would start with a credit of approximately $74 at payment 120. It's not long before this initial $50 increase in principal starts to accelerate and completely offset the $900 cost.

The Cliftons could also go one step further, borrowing the entire $11,351 upgrade and eliminating all 15 years of payments at once. Trading one debt for another, more favorable debt is common among real estate professionals, but there's no guarantee it will work for you. The only way to determine whether borrowing extra money will work is to break out a pencil and calculate the impact of a lump sum payment, including the fact that the interest on the commercial bank loan may no longer be tax-deductible.

Trading one kind of debt for another has as many wrinkles as your imagination allows. For instance, you can even get *extra credit* for making a lump sum payment ahead of schedule. For example, if you have a balloon mortgage held by a private party and not due for several years, it may be in the private party's best interest to give you a bonus if you make a lump sum payment ahead of schedule. This can be especially valuable because, as you know, a small decrease in the outstanding loan balance can save a very large amount of scheduled interest expense. The exact amount of the bonus is subject to negotiation. However, there are "future value" tables that are used to calculate the premium on this money. You can ask any accountant or financial adviser to compute the premium you should receive for paying ahead of schedule.

These are just a few ideas for where you can get the extra money for the prepayment. There are many, many more. In the final analysis no source is more important than your determination to succeed. It's as Earl Nightingale said: "Every man is self-made. Only the successful will admit it."

House Shopping

The best way to shop for a house is to know the borrowing power of your monthly payment *before* you start looking at houses. Knowing how much you can borrow at the different repayment terms gives you the insight to choose a house that satisfies your desire yet encourages you to take a mortgage that is 5, 10, or even 15 years shorter than the traditional 30-year mortgage. Taking a shorter-term mortgage saves an awesome amount of interest expense while sacrificing only a small amount of borrowing and buying power.

Unfortunately, most people go about it just the other way; they find the house first and learn if their monthly payment can borrow enough money afterward. Consequently, many people automatically take a 30-year mortgage and pay a huge amount of unnecessary interest expense. They don't realize, for instance, that the difference in the borrowing power of their monthly payment between a 20-year and a 30-year mortgage may be only 8 percent of their total borrowing power. For example, the Cliftons' $666.63 mortgage payment at 11 percent would pay off a $64,600 mortgage in 20 years. Instead they bought a $70,000 house that required a 30-year mortgage. The difference between the two mortgages amounts to a mere $5,400. The cost of that additional $5,400 is a staggering $74,000 in additional interest expense. The additional $5,400 may have purchased nothing more than a set of new kitchen cabinets in the more expensive house. Nice as they might be, no one would pay $74,000 in additional interest expense if they knew that this was the true cost of those cabinets. They would buy the less expensive house instead.

It's even more dramatic between a 25-year and 30-year mortgage. The borrowing power is increased a mere $1,985, while the interest expense is an additional $38,000. Furthermore, this additional expense doesn't even consider the loss of the opportunity to do something else with your money for 5 or 10 years. That something else may be a savings account, retiring 10 years earlier, or investing in a business that you've always wanted to start.

These are the kind of unnecessary mistakes that can be avoided by shopping for a house with a chart on the borrowing power of your monthly payment stuffed into your back pocket. If you are a prospective home buyer who turned to this chapter before reading the rest of the book, there is a shortcut for learning your borrowing power: call your real estate or lending institution. They can generally compute your borrowing power in a matter of minutes.

The first step in learning your borrowing power is to arrange it with the shortest term first and increase it by five-year increments.

Table 30

Borrowing Power at 11 Percent: The Cliftons

Term (Years)	Borrowing Power
5	$30,655
10	48,391
15	58,650
20	64,584
25	68,016
30	70,000

Obviously the majority of your borrowing power is in the shorter terms of the mortgage. Each five-year increase in the term yields less and less borrowing power, until the last increase yields virtually nothing.

Now that you know the amounts of your borrowing power, it's a good idea to know the total amount of mortgage payments required to pay off that borrowing power. This is accomplished by multiplying the monthly payment by the 60 months in a 5-year term. For example, the scheduled payments on the Cliftons' mortgage are $39,998 ($666.63 multiplied by 60 months).

Table 31

**Borrowing Power and Total Payments at 11 Percent:
The Cliftons**

Term (Years)	Borrowing Power	Total Payments
5	$30,655	$ 39,998
10	48,391	79,996
15	58,650	119,994
20	64,584	159,992
25	68,016	199,990
30	70,000	239,988

This is a good, simple, yet extremely powerful chart. It can help you select a house that satisfies your desire but that may require only a 20-year mortgage instead of a 30-year one.

You can get as fancy and precise as you wish. Rather than eyeballing the difference between your borrowing power at the different terms and its increasing cost, you can construct a couple of more columns and specify the exact dollar increase in borrowing power between the various five-year periods. As used earlier, these increases are sometimes called the *upgrade*. You can also specify the "penalty" in terms of additional interest expense for that upgrade. The value of being so precise is to leave nothing to chance.

Shopping for a home, which is probably your biggest investment, with a borrowing power chart in your pocket is planning ahead like a professional. Professional real estate investors realize there are two halves to a real estate investment: the *getting in* half and the *getting out* half. They know that getting the mortgage is only one part of the equation, the easy part. Paying it off is the second part, the hard part. Realizing that their success is keyed to getting out of an investment is why most professionals use devices such as borrowing power charts. They know if they can visualize how they will successfully get out of an investment before they ever get into it, their chances of a successful venture are greatly enhanced. You can follow their lead by preparing your own borrowing power chart and making your decisions like a pro.

New Mortgages

Another example of planning ahead is researching new loan programs such as the biweekly mortgage. The biweekly mortgage, which was very successful in Canada before making its debut in America, cuts 10 or 12 years off a 30-year mortgage. It does so by reducing the outstanding balance twice a month, instead of the standard once a month, and because it also pays the equivalent of 13 monthly payments. Even though there are some catches that you should be aware of, the biweekly mortgage is a positive step in helping homeowners buy equity ownership as quickly and cheaply as possible.

This is how it works: every two weeks the homeowner makes a payment that is half the size of the normal monthly payment. For example, if the Cliftons had a biweekly mortgage, they would pay $348.45 every two weeks instead of $666.63 every month. Since the outstanding balance is reduced by a small amount every two weeks, the amount of interest due on the next payment will be slightly lower. Although the amount of reduction is slight, the impact is great. It's like a slow drip in the bathtub—before you know it the tub is overflowing.

The other reason the biweekly mortgage is paid off ahead of schedule is that there are 52 weeks in a year, so you will actually make 26 biweekly payments. Accordingly, two additional payments of $348.45 each are made every calendar year. This equals 13 monthly payments, reducing the balance even further. More frequent payments and the extra payments against principal are the two reasons that an 11 percent 30-year mortgage is paid off in approximately 20 years.

A couple words of caution about the biweekly mortgage program: Biweekly payments must be made for the entire 20 years of the program. This can get awfully tiring, especially when you consider that virtually all of the saving has been accomplished in the early years of the program. This means that the last 10 years of the program are an utter waste of time and money. Furthermore, it implies that you intend to be in the same house for as many as 20 years. This may not be totally realistic, since statistics indicate that 5 years is about the average that most people stay in the same house. Therefore, they won't realize the supposed rewards of the biweekly method.

The other word of caution concerns the power of the lender to cancel the biweekly mortgage. The biweekly plan calls for the mortgage payment to be debited directly against a checking account. Should you have insufficient funds in the account, the lender may cancel the program at its discretion. The exact number of times this must occur before the cancellation privilege is exercised varies according to the lender. Check the loan document thoroughly for these and any other features unique to the biweekly mortgage.

Despite these drawbacks, the biweekly mortgage has become popular among people who are in the lead of long-term trends. These are the same people who made a virtue out of debt back in the 1970s and early 1980s. They have concluded that debt is no longer profitable and have turned to building equity ownership at the lowest possible cost as the new way to preserve their lifestyle. The demand for the biweekly mortgage is so strong among this group that it often accounts for 50 percent of all the loans made by lending institutions that offer them. Furthermore, these loans are typically considered to be of the highest quality because demographically the borrowers rank in the top categories of income, education, occupation, neighborhood, and so forth. Accordingly, lending institutions are delighted to have them as customers. The only reason that more lenders don't offer the biweekly program is that they don't have the equipment or people to handle two payments a month. Usually only savings and loan companies can accommodate the added servicing requirements; therefore they comprise the majority of lenders offering the biweekly program.

The biweekly mortgage is but one discovery you may make when researching new opportunities and planning ahead. Unfortunately, you have to do this pretty much on your own, because only a few mortgage advisers earn their money independently of lending institutions. But the research effort may be highly rewarded. The latest program currently being tested in Canada is the "paycheck mortgage." Many Canadians are paid weekly. The paycheck mortgage is designed to be paid weekly and thus is retired even more quickly than is the biweekly mortgage. Who knows? Perhaps we'll see the paycheck mortgage in the United States before long.

Refinancing

This chapter wouldn't be complete without a discussion of the best way to refinance or, more precisely, the best way to build equity ownership through refinancing.

Many people consider refinancing as a way to lower their monthly payment. Actually the best purpose of refinancing is to reduce the true cost of buying a home. The "true cost" of a mortgage is the total amount of cash required to repay the original loan balance—in short, the cost to buy ownership. Since it's the length of the repayment term that adds the greatest amount of interest expense, I look first at refinancing in terms of reducing the term of the mortgage, not the monthly payment.

For example, if the Cliftons have the opportunity to lower their mortgage by 2 percent, they have the choice of converting that 2 percent into a lower monthly payment or reducing the term of their mortgage. Table 32 presents those options:

Table 32

Reduction in Repayment Term

Rate	Decrease	Term (Years)	Monthly Payment
10.5	.5%	24.00	$640.32
10.0	1.0	21.00	614.31
9.5	1.5	19.00	588.60
9.0	2.0	17.25	563.24

As you can see from Table 32, a reduction in the interest rate from 11 percent to 9 percent reduces the term of the mortgage to almost 17 years. This means almost 13 years have been cut off the repayment schedule. Thirteen years' worth of payments at $666.63 per month amount to a savings of about $104,000. Also, you can earn interest income on those 13 years of ex–mortgage payments.

A homeowner who chooses the other route lowers the monthly payment to $563.24 and saves $103.39 per month. Choosing to save $103.39 per month over the $104,000 grand savings is a classic case of being penny-wise and dollar-foolish.

There is, however, the opportunity to win both ways. If the rate drops far enough, you can reduce both the term of the mortgage and the monthly payment. For example, my sister and her husband, Eileen and Joe, whom you may recall from the Preface, started with a $28,000 14.875 percent 30-year mortgage. They first made a lump sum prepayment of $3,000 and immediately saved $59,000 of scheduled interest expense, eliminating 15 years of payments. Several years later the rates receded to 9.5 percent, so they refinanced, took a new 10-year mortgage, and also reduced their monthly payment. They got it all!

One reason they received such a dramatic reduction was that the rates had fallen almost 5 percent. Another reason was their additional equity in the house. First, the earlier lump sum prepayment added $3,000 of equity, and second, their subsequent normal monthly payments were receiving a healthy amount of credit toward principal. When it came time to refinance, their outstanding balance was substantially lower, and the combined lower interest rate allowed them both to reduce the term and to lower the monthly payment.

Theirs is a classic case of never returning to a 30-year mortgage but parlaying each new mortgage opportunity into a shorter and shorter term. They started with a 30-year mortgage in 1982 and by 1988 had only 9 years of indebtedness left on their home. Their home will be completely paid off by the time their daughter, Kelly, is in fifth grade. They can start a nest egg at that point and be fairly confident that they'll have a good share of her college tuition put aside by the time she's ready.

Pitfalls

There are several "do not" rules that I would like to pass along. Do not take a negative amortization mortgage, sometimes called a *neutron mortgage*. It's called a neutron mortgage because the house is left standing intact but the homeowner gets wiped out. These so-called negative amortization loans are deadly. The incentive for negative amortization mortgages is that the monthly payment is artificially low, which enables some people to afford homes that they couldn't purchase otherwise. Unfortunately, the difference between the real interest rate and the actual monthly payment is added back to the loan balance, and it grows larger with time. Unless there is a sufficient amount of appreciation to offset the rising loan balance, the homeowner eventually gets wiped out.

As an example, if the Cliftons were to pay only $600.00 per month, instead of the $666.63 they really owed, the outstanding balance would be almost $74,000 after five years of mortgage payment. Thus they would go more deeply into debt the longer they had a negative amortization loan. The hope with such loans is that appreciation will bail the homeowner out. But what happens when appreciation is fickle enough to fade away, and the mortgage comes due? What happens is the homeowner is wiped out.

The language on these loans can also be tricky. Some advertisements state that the payments won't go up but are silent on whether the actual interest rate is increasing. And in fact it usually is. The difference between the payment and the actual rate, which is unannounced, is actually added to the principal loan balance. This means that the homeowner goes deeper into the hole.

Fortunately, the lending industry has realized the danger of negative amortization mortgages and has taken steps to curb their worst features. Lenders realize that mass foreclosures are in no one's best interest, and they are working to stop this practice before more people get hurt.

Although negative amortization loans are the worst example of creative financing run amok, you are well advised to be wary of creative financing in general. Creative financing does nothing other than buy time. The fundamental problems do not go away. They are merely put on ice in hope that the situation will become more advantageous. Time sometimes solves the problem, but other times it only adds to it.

Balloon mortgages, an excellent example of creative financing, became a stopgap measure in the late 1970s and early 1980s as the combined cost of housing and financing made home ownership financially impossible for many people. A balloon mortgage is essentially short-term financing that allows a sale to take place so a seller and a buyer realize their immediate objective. The problem with a balloon mortgage is twofold. First, it assumes that the situation will be sufficiently better in 3, 5, 7, or even 10 years, so that permanent financing may be obtained. Assuming the situation will get better is throwing your fate to chance, for it may get better or it may also get worse. No one can possibly know for sure. Second, a balloon mortgage does not assume that it will be fully amortized. Even after a relatively long 10-year balloon mortgage, 95 percent of the original balance is still outstanding. This means that the average homeowner will take a new 30-year mortgage, return to "Go," and start the whole process all over again. The 10 years of mortgage payments are essentially wasted. Balloons may be mighty tempting, especially on that dream house, but the general rule of thumb is to avoid any financing scheme that gets you into a house but leaves you with no way to get out.

A Last Word and Heading On . . .

There's one part of this entire prepayment program that is irreplaceable, and that's your active participation. The custom prepayment plan can't do it all for you; it needs your creativity and energy to live up to its potential. Furthermore, the basic strategy and tactics that were outlined in the previous chapters are only the minimum. If you put your mind to it and improve on some of the tips offered in this chapter, you can actually save more money and pay off your mortgage earlier than in the standard custom plan.

The next chapter is titled "A Last Word" because it's time to turn off the lights over my desk and turn the program over to you. There's only one thing left for me to do, and that is to remind you that only change is eternal and home is sacred space. Safeguarding the sacred space by building real equity ownership and a nest egg of your own is a plan that you can bet your life on.

10
A Last Word

I t's been said that life is like a journey in a rowboat, you can see the past and present, but your back is toward the future. That may be true, but it still doesn't prevent us from navigating down the river of life. All we need to do is take notice of the changing landscape, keep an eye on the weather, and follow the current. The rest will take care of itself.

It matters little whether you choose an equity-wise mortgage from the start, prepay your mortgage, or adopt a principal acceleration strategy. Nor does it matter whether your plans are pinpoint accurate or not. What really matters is that you adopt an equity strategy. A nest egg is sure to follow.

Furthermore, money isn't nearly the controlling factor that most people think it is. Most people actually manage their financial affairs according to what they believe to be true and important in life, not according to financial techniques. Beliefs and value systems lead; techniques follow. Those who believe in safety, for instance, don't also believe in risky propositions. Similarly, those who believe in saving money don't also try to keep up with the Jones family.

Indeed, belief in the value of a nest egg is more important than financial information and techniques in building it. In other words, it is the commitment of the heart that leads, and information and techniques that follow.

No place is this more true than the home. Home holds a special place in our hearts. Intuitively, people know it's their sanctuary. They also know their sense of well-being and happiness is connected with home. No other place provides the same peace, sanctity, and security. Home is sacred space.

That's why, in addition to all the "how to" tools, my intention was to provide a fresh vision of your home sanctuary. I hope I've succeeded. In any event, my job is finished. Now it's up to you. As someone else said, "Life is like a clipper, only you can be the skipper."

Index

236　How to Unscramble Your Nest Egg

Repayment schedule
negative amortization
  mortgages and, 226
opportunity loss and, 81–82
parallel track strategy and, 83,
  84–85
Mortgage prepayment, xii,
  149–70, 196–211
communication and, 198
credit date and, 202–3
debt myth on affordability of,
  173, 177
described, 93–94
eliminating payments in,
  153–54
midmonth budget adjustment
  and, 154–58
missing prepayments and,
  152–53
notification of, 199
number of checks for, 201, 202
outstanding balance
  verification in, 205–6
payment amount in, 152
planning in, 206–10
prepayment clauses, 199
reasons for effectiveness of,
  98–104
records of, 203–5
working with lenders in,
  196–98
Mortgage tables. *See* Standard
  mortgage tables
Mortgages, 221–24
biweekly, 221–23
paycheck, 223–24
selecting equity-wise, 58, 59–80
5-year, 93
10-year. *See* 10-year mortgage
15-year. *See* 15-year mortgage
20-year. *See* 20-year mortgage
25-year, 77, 79, 219
30-year. *See* 30-year mortgage
40-year, 84
Moving, debt myth on, 173,
  177–79

National Association of Realtors,
  194
National debt, 181
Nazi party, 182
Negative amortization (neutron)
  mortgages, 226–27

Next-month principal method, 96,
  120
Nightingale, Earl, 218
Noriega, Manuel, 21
Nothing down, debt myth on, 174,
  189
Notification, 199

Opportunity loss, 58, 73, 75–80,
  85–86. *See also* Initial gain
5-year plan and, 106
mortgage prepayment and, 101
parallel track strategy and, 85
principal acceleration and,
  104–5, 109, 113
shortcut to determining, 81–82
Outstanding balance verification,
  205–6

Parallel track strategy, 83–85
Parlaying, 183
Passover, 17
Pay yourself first philosophy,
  90–93, 102
Paycheck mortgages, 223–24
Paying in arrears, 139
Payoff, debt myth on, 173, 187–88
Peace, 13–16
Peck, M. Scott, 5
Pension plans, 40–41
Pink zone, 60, 61
defined, 59
interest expense and, 59, 70, 71
opportunity loss and, 76, 77, 86
purchasing power and, 63
Planning, 206–10
Plumbing analogy, 80–81
Points
defined, 85
mortgage prepayment and, 197
parallel track strategy and,
  84–85
Power of Myth, The (Campbell), 4
Prepayment clauses, 199
Prepayment penalty, debt myth
  on, 174, 189–91
Prime interest rate, 45
Principal
amortization schedule and, 122
constant payment method and,
  95
conversion tables and, 123–25
credited to payments, 188

ORDER FORM

Equity-Wise Mortgage Software

Name _____

Address _____

Unit or Suite _____ City/State/Zip _____

Phone: Day _____ Evening _____

Price*	$19.95	*Price subject to change without prior notification.
Shipping	2.50	
Tax (Colorado residents only)	1.80	
Subtotal	_____	
Add'l. Orders	_____	
Total	_____	

☐ Enclosed is my check or money order.

Charge my: ☐ Visa ☐ MasterCard ☐ AmEx

☐ Other _____

Card Number _____ Exp. Date _____

Signature _____

Specify one: ☐ DOS ☐ Apple

System Requirements: 256K or higher.
Both 5.25″ and 3.5″ disks included.

Send order to: Cunningham Advisors
730 17th St., Suite 450
Denver, CO 80202

ORDER FORM
Equity-Wise Mortgage Software

Name _____

Address _____

Unit or Suite _____ City/State/Zip _____

Phone: Day _____ Evening _____

Price*	$19.95	*Price subject to change without prior notification.
Shipping	2.50	
Tax (Colorado residents only)	1.80	
Subtotal	_____	
Add'l. Orders	_____	
Total	_____	

☐ Enclosed is my check or money order.

Charge my: ☐ Visa ☐ MasterCard ☐ AmEx

☐ Other _____

Card Number _____ Exp. Date _____

Signature _____

Specify one: ☐ DOS ☐ Apple

System Requirements: 256K or higher.
Both 5.25" and 3.5" disks included.

Send order to: Cunningham Advisors
730 17th St., Suite 450
Denver, CO 80202